STUDY PLANNER

CHAPTER 01 **문장의 구조**	학습일	
UNIT 01	월	일
UNIT 02	월	일
Review Test	월	일

CHAPTER 07 **관계사**	학습일	
UNIT 13	월	일
UNIT 14	월	일
UNIT 15	월	일
Review Test	월	일

CHAPTER 02 **to부정사**	학습일	
UNIT 03	월	일
UNIT 04	월	일
Review Test	월	일

CHAPTER 08 **비교 구문**	학습일	
UNIT 16	월	일
UNIT 17	월	일
Review Test	월	일

CHAPTER 03 **동명사**	학습일	
UNIT 05	월	일
UNIT 06	월	일
Review Test	월	일

CHAPTER 09 **분사**	학습일	
UNIT 18	월	일
UNIT 19	월	일
Review Test	월	일

CHAPTER 04 **시제**	학습일	
UNIT 07	월	일
UNIT 08	월	일
Review Test	월	일

CHAPTER 10 **접속사**	학습일	
UNIT 20	월	일
UNIT 21	월	일
Review Test	월	일

CHAPTER 05 **조동사**	학습일	
UNIT 09	월	일
UNIT 10	월	일
Review Test	월	일

CHAPTER 11 **가정법**	학습일	
UNIT 22	월	일
UNIT 23	월	일
Review Test	월	일

CHAPTER 06 **수동태**	학습일	
UNIT 11	월	일
UNIT 12	월	일
Review Test	월	일

CHAPTER 12 **특수 구문**	학습일	
UNIT 24	월	일
UNIT 25	월	일
Review Test	월	일

SCORECARD

CHAPTER 01 문장의 구조	점수	PASS
UNIT 01	/ 30점	26점
UNIT 02	/ 30점	26점
Review Test	/ 60점	51점

CHAPTER 07 관계사	점수	PASS
UNIT 13	/ 30점	26점
UNIT 14	/ 30점	26점
UNIT 15	/ 25점	22점
Review Test	/ 70점	60점

CHAPTER 02 to부정사	점수	PASS
UNIT 03	/ 30점	26점
UNIT 04	/ 25점	22점
Review Test	/ 60점	51점

CHAPTER 08 비교 구문	점수	PASS
UNIT 16	/ 30점	26점
UNIT 17	/ 25점	22점
Review Test	/ 60점	51점

CHAPTER 03 동명사	점수	PASS
UNIT 05	/ 30점	26점
UNIT 06	/ 30점	26점
Review Test	/ 70점	60점

CHAPTER 09 분사	점수	PASS
UNIT 18	/ 35점	30점
UNIT 19	/ 25점	22점
Review Test	/ 60점	51점

CHAPTER 04 시제	점수	PASS
UNIT 07	/ 30점	26점
UNIT 08	/ 25점	22점
Review Test	/ 60점	51점

CHAPTER 10 접속사	점수	PASS
UNIT 20	/ 25점	22점
UNIT 21	/ 25점	22점
Review Test	/ 70점	60점

CHAPTER 05 조동사	점수	PASS
UNIT 09	/ 25점	22점
UNIT 10	/ 25점	22점
Review Test	/ 60점	51점

CHAPTER 11 가정법	점수	PASS
UNIT 22	/ 25점	22점
UNIT 23	/ 25점	22점
Review Test	/ 60점	51점

CHAPTER 06 수동태	점수	PASS
UNIT 11	/ 30점	26점
UNIT 12	/ 30점	26점
Review Test	/ 60점	51점

CHAPTER 12 특수 구문	점수	PASS
UNIT 24	/ 25점	22점
UNIT 25	/ 25점	22점
Review Test	/ 60점	51점

내신공략

중학영문법

개념이해책

3

내신공략 중학영문법의 구성 및 특징

시리즈 구성

내신공략 중학영문법 시리즈는 중학교 영어 교과과정의 문법 사항을 3레벨로 나누어 수록하고 있으며, 각각의 레벨은 **개념이해책**과 **문제풀이책**으로 구성됩니다. 두 책을 병행하여 학습하는 것이 가장 이상적인 학습법이지만, 교사와 학생의 필요에 따라 둘 중 하나만을 독립적으로도 사용할 수 있도록 구성했습니다.

개념이해책은 문법 개념에 대한 핵심적인 설명과 필수 연습문제로 이루어져 있습니다.

문제풀이책은 각 문법 개념에 대해 총 3단계의 테스트를 통해 체계적으로 문제를 풀어볼 수 있도록 구성되어 있습니다.

특징

❶ 최신 내신 출제 경향 100% 반영

– 신유형과 고난도 서술형 문제 비중 강화

점점 어려워지는 내신 문제의 최신 경향을 철저히 분석·반영하여 고난도 서술형과 신유형 문제의 비중을 더욱 높였습니다. 이 책으로 학습한 학생들은 어떤 유형의 문제에도 대처할 수 있습니다.

– 영어 지시문 문제 제시

영어로 문제가 출제되는 최신 경향을 반영하여, 일부 문제를 영어 지시문으로 제시했습니다. 문제풀이책의 Level 3 Test는 모두 영어 지시문으로만 제시됩니다.

– 독해 지문 어법 문제 수록(문제풀이책)

독해 지문에서 어법 문제가 출제되는 내신 문제 스타일에 익숙해지도록, 독해 지문과 함께 다양한 어법 문제를 풀어볼 수 있습니다.

❷ 개념이해책과 문제풀이책의 연계 학습

문법 개념 설명과 필수 문제로 구성된 개념이해책으로 문법 개념을 학습한 후, 다양한 문제를 3단계로 풀어보는 문제풀이책으로 복습하며 확실한 학습 효과를 거둘 수 있습니다.

❸ 성취도 평가와 수준별 맞춤형 학습 제안

문제를 풀어보고 나서 점수 기준에 따라 학생의 성취도를 평가할 수 있습니다. 개념이해책에서 Let's Check It Out과 Ready for Exams 점수를 합산한 결과에 따라 문제풀이책의 어느 레벨부터 학습하면 되는지 가이드가 제시됩니다. Review Test에서는 일정 점수 이상을 받아야 다음 챕터로 넘어갈 수 있습니다.

❹ 추가 학습을 위한 다양한 학습자료 제공

다양하게 수업에 활용할 수 있는 교사용 자료가 제공됩니다. 다락원 홈페이지(www.darakwon.co.kr)에서 무료로 다운받으실 수 있습니다.

개념이해책과 문제풀이책 연계 학습법

개념이해책으로 문법 개념 학습

문제풀이책으로 문법 개념을 복습

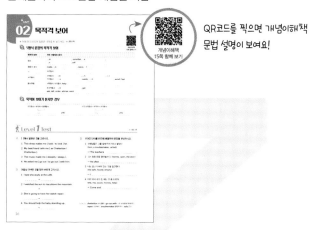

QR코드를 찍으면 개념이해책 문법 설명이 보여요!

개념이해책 Let's Check It Out과 Ready for Exams 풀고 점수 합산

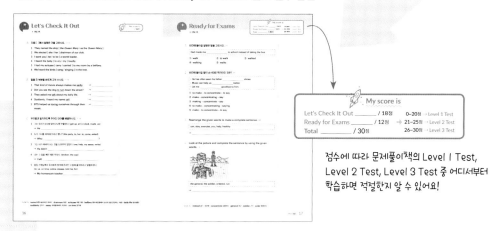

점수에 따라 문제풀이책의 Level 1 Test, Level 2 Test, Level 3 Test 중 어디서부터 학습하면 적절한지 알 수 있어요!

챕터 내용을 모두 학습한 후 Review Test 풀기

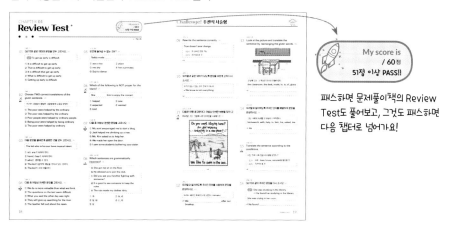

패스하면 문제풀이책의 Review Test도 풀어보고, 그것도 패스하면 다음 챕터로 넘어가요!

개념이해책의 구성

문법 개념 설명

문법 항목에 대한 핵심 내용이 개념(Concept)별로 간결하게 정리되어 있습니다. 표와 도식을 통해 내용을 한눈에 파악하기 쉽습니다.

● Grammar Point
학생들이 잘 모르는 중요한 내용을 꼼꼼하게 짚고 넘어갈 수 있습니다.

● VOCA
예문에 쓰인 주요 단어가 정리되어 편리하며, 문법과 단어 공부를 같이 할 수 있습니다.

Let's Check It Out

Ready for Exams

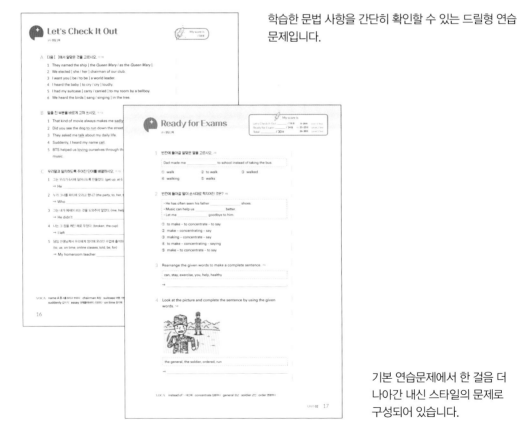

학습한 문법 사항을 간단히 확인할 수 있는 드릴형 연습 문제입니다.

기본 연습문제에서 한 걸음 더 나아간 내신 스타일의 문제로 구성되어 있습니다.

Review Test

챕터 학습이 끝나면 내신 시험 유형의 문제를 풀어보며 배운 내용을 정리합니다. 챕터 내 여러 유닛의 내용을 통합적으로 구성한 문제를 통해 응용력과 실전 감각을 키울 수 있습니다.

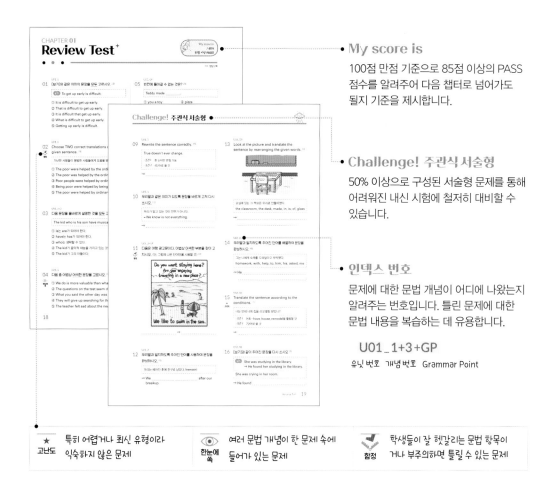

My score is
100점 만점 기준으로 85점 이상의 PASS 점수를 알려주어 다음 챕터로 넘어가도 될지 기준을 제시합니다.

Challenge! 주관식 서술형
50% 이상으로 구성된 서술형 문제를 통해 어려워진 내신 시험에 철저히 대비할 수 있습니다.

인덱스 번호
문제에 대한 문법 개념이 어디에 나왔는지 알려주는 번호입니다. 틀린 문제에 대한 문법 내용을 복습하는 데 유용합니다.

U01_1+3+GP
유닛 번호 개념 번호 Grammar Point

★ **고난도** 특히 어렵거나 최신 유형이라 익숙하지 않은 문제

👁 **한눈에 쏙** 여러 문법 개념이 한 문제 속에 들어가 있는 문제

✓ **함정** 학생들이 잘 헷갈리는 문법 항목이거나 부주의하면 틀릴 수 있는 문제

시험 직전에 챙겨 보는 비법 노트

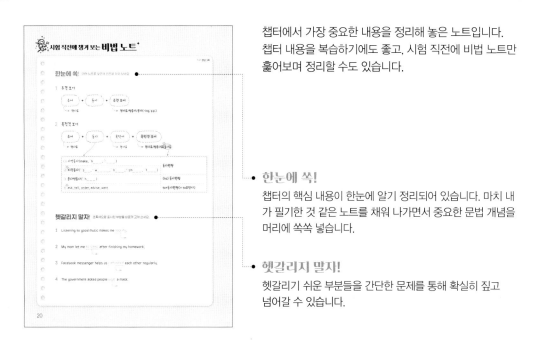

챕터에서 가장 중요한 내용을 정리해 놓은 노트입니다. 챕터 내용을 복습하기에도 좋고, 시험 직전에 비법 노트만 훑어보며 정리할 수도 있습니다.

한눈에 쏙!
챕터의 핵심 내용이 한눈에 알기 정리되어 있습니다. 마치 내가 필기한 것 같은 노트를 채워 나가면서 중요한 문법 개념을 머리에 쏙쏙 넣습니다.

헷갈리지 말자!
헷갈리기 쉬운 부분들을 간단한 문제를 통해 확실히 짚고 넘어갈 수 있습니다.

차례

CHAPTER 01 **문장의 구조**   11

UNIT 01 주어, 목적어, 주격 보어
UNIT 02 목적격 보어
Review Test
시험 직전에 챙겨 보는 비법 노트

CHAPTER 02 **to부정사**   21

UNIT 03 용법, 의미상의 주어, 부정
UNIT 04 시제, 독립부정사, 대부정사
Review Test
시험 직전에 챙겨 보는 비법 노트

CHAPTER 03 **동명사**   31

UNIT 05 용법, 의미상의 주어, 부정
UNIT 06 동명사, 현재분사, to부정사
Review Test
시험 직전에 챙겨 보는 비법 노트

CHAPTER 04 **시제**   41

UNIT 07 단순 시제, 현재완료 시제
UNIT 08 과거완료 시제, 진행 시제
Review Test
시험 직전에 챙겨 보는 비법 노트

CHAPTER 05 **조동사**   51

UNIT 09 조동사(1)
UNIT 10 조동사(2)
Review Test
시험 직전에 챙겨 보는 비법 노트

CHAPTER 06 **수동태**   61

UNIT 11 조동사, 진행형, 완료형의 수동태
UNIT 12 여러 가지 수동태
Review Test
시험 직전에 챙겨 보는 비법 노트

CHAPTER 07 관계사   71

UNIT 13 관계대명사의 역할과 용법
UNIT 14 관계부사, 관계사의 생략
UNIT 15 복합관계사
Review Test
시험 직전에 챙겨 보는 비법 노트

CHAPTER 08 비교 구문   85

UNIT 16 비교 변화, 원급 이용 비교 구문
UNIT 17 비교급, 최상급 구문
Review Test
시험 직전에 챙겨 보는 비법 노트

CHAPTER 09 분사   95

UNIT 18 분사
UNIT 19 분사구문
Review Test
시험 직전에 챙겨 보는 비법 노트

CHAPTER 10 접속사   105

UNIT 20 등위 접속사, 상관 접속사, 종속 접속사
UNIT 21 종속 접속사
Review Test
시험 직전에 챙겨 보는 비법 노트

CHAPTER 11 가정법   115

UNIT 22 가정법 과거, 가정법 과거완료
UNIT 23 I wish 가정법, as if 가정법
Review Test
시험 직전에 챙겨 보는 비법 노트

CHAPTER 12 특수 구문   125

UNIT 24 강조, 생략
UNIT 25 도치
Review Test
시험 직전에 챙겨 보는 비법 노트

불규칙 동사 변화표   135

최고의 수업은 학생들이 최고로 쉽게 이해하고 기억하는 수업이듯 최고의 책도 결국은 이해하고 기억하기 쉬운 책이 아닐까 싶다. 내공 중학영문법은 개념 설명이 간결하여 이해하기 쉽고 실제 시험에 출제되는 신유형의 문제들로 구성되어 학생들의 실전 시험에 직접적인 도움이 된다는 꾸준한 호평을 받고 있는 책이다.

대치동 학원 원장 **유니스 리**

유명 출판사의 여러 문법 교재 제작에 참여했지만 지루하고 어려운 영문법을 어떻게 맛깔나게 구현할 것인가가 늘 품었던 난제였다. 재치가 번뜩이는 예문, 간결하고 깔끔한 설명, 학습자에게 가장 효율적인 동선을 제시해 타 교재는 그냥 평범하게 만들어 버리는 내공 중학영문법만의 마법을 부리고 있는 듯하다.

파주 너희가별이다 원장 **최현진**

교재를 선택하는 데 있어서 '티칭' 입장과 '학생' 입장을 모두 고려했을 때 편한 책을 선택하는데요. 어려워 보이거나 문제가 많거나 했을 때는 쉽게 포기할 수도 있는 부분이 있어서 매번 책을 볼 때는 중점적으로 보는 편입니다. 내공 중학영문법은 문법 학습과 필수 기출 유형은 개념이해책을 통해서 학습하고, 이러한 개념을 문제풀이책에서 다시 한 번 되새길 수 있어서 매우 좋습니다. 고등학교 가기 전, 필수 잇템 교재로 생각됩니다.

태안 박쌤영어 강사 **박희진**

개념이해책에서 문법을 배우며 수업 중에 함께 문제를 풀고, 워크북 개념의 문제풀이책에서 문제들뿐만 아니라 표 형식의 문법 정리 내용 역시 암기하도록 구성되어서, 학생들이 문법 내용을 덩어리로 익힐 수 있다. 저자들의 창의성이 돋보이는 풍부한 양의 학교 시험 대비 up-to-date한 신유형 문제들과 영어 몰입 교육이 가능한 영어로 출제되는 문제들 역시 이 책의 장점이다.

마포 껌학원 원장 **김현우**

내공 중학영문법으로 공부를 한 후, 37점이었던 처참한 점수가 90점 가량으로 많이 올라갔습니다. 이 책에서는 문법에 대해 상세하고 정확하게 알려주고 있으니 저처럼 기초가 없이 영어 공부를 시작하는 중학생이라면 이 책을 써보는 걸 추천합니다.

경성중학교 3학년 05년생 **신경○**

이 책으로 강의를 하면서 문법은 무조건 많이 풀어야 한다는 기존의 생각을 완전히 버리게 되었다. 개념 정리부터 기본 문제, 심화 문제까지 알차게 구성되어 있어 아이들이 어느 부분에서 이해가 부족한지 정확하게 찾아낼 수 있다. 특히 문제풀이책은 난이도별로 문제를 단순하게 모아둔 문제은행의 개념이 아니라, 이전 단계의 핵심 문제를 적절히 업그레이드해서 어느 유형에서도 응용이 가능하게 했다. 수록된 문제의 유형 역시 흔하지 않은 구성으로 되어 있어 대충 풀고 넘어가기에는 함정이 많다. 그래서 이 책을 선택하는 아이들은 정말 '제대로' 된 영어 공부를 하게 된다. 개념을 단계별로 정리하는 것부터 문제의 양과 질, 그리고 부가자료까지 버릴 게 하나도 없는 주옥 같은 책이다.

여의도/마포 강사 김경민

개념이해책과 문제풀이책이 같이 있어 문제의 양이 부족하지 않았고 난이도가 잘 나눠져 있어서 내가 어느 위치에 있는지 파악하며 쉽게 문법을 배울 수 있었다. 문법 문제를 항상 어설프게 느낌으로만 풀던 내가 이 책으로 공부를 하고 나서는 이 문제가 어떤 개념을 물어보는 것인지, 정답의 근거가 무엇인지 잘 설명할 수 있게 되었다.

여의도중학교 최민준

누가 봐도 알기 쉽고 접근하기 쉽게 책이 구성되어 있다. 그리고 요즘 학생들의 관심사를 배려한 모든 예문과 답문의 단어가 정성스럽게 선택되어 있는 점에 감탄했다. 힘든 영어 공부를 하는 학생을 최고로 배려해 만들어진 교재임을 한눈에 알 수 있다.

미국 국공립 학교 교사 20년차 Reena Han

고난도 문제도 쉽게 풀 수 있도록 다양한 난이도의 풍부한 문제 수와 고퀄리티의 문제들이 가득해서 문법을 확실하게 익힐 수 있는, 엄청난 내공이 담긴 교재!♡

중계 Amy English 원장 장여주

영문법에 예외가 많아서 항상 한계에 도달하는 느낌을 받았었는데 신영주 선생님과 이 책으로 공부하면서 내가 정확히 알지 못해서 예외라고 느끼고 외우려고 했다는 점을 깨달을 수 있었습니다. 그 동안 수많은 문제집을 풀면서 가졌던 크고 작은 질문에 대해서도 명쾌한 답을 제시해주었고 이러한 성취의 경험을 통해 사소한 의문도 지나치지 않는 공부 습관을 잡을 수 있었습니다. 교재를 접하는 학생의 수준과 상관없이 실력을 향상시키는 데 반드시 도움이 되는 책이라고 생각합니다.

외대부고 13기 배현진

CHAPTER 01
문장의 구조

UNIT 01   **주어, 목적어, 주격 보어**

UNIT 02   **목적격 보어**

UNIT 01 주어, 목적어, 주격 보어

1 주어의 이해

주어(~은/는/이/가)가 될 수 있는 것은 명사 상당어구이다.

명사		A puppy is under the table.
명사구	to부정사구	To blame others is easy.
	동명사구	Shopping with mobile apps is convenient.
	the+형용사	The rich grow richer, and the poor grow poorer.
	의문사+to부정사	How to study is more important than what to study.
명사절	that절	That the pen is mightier than the sword is true.
	whether절	Whether you believe it or not is up to you.
	의문사절	Where we will stay has not been decided yet.
	what절	What we want is peace.

2 목적어의 이해

목적어(~을/를/에게)가 될 수 있는 것은 명사 상당어구이다.

명사		We admire Yi Sun-sin.
명사구	to부정사구	Scientists want to prevent infectious diseases.
	동명사구	We enjoy riding our bikes.
	the+형용사	The volunteers helped the homeless.
	의문사+to부정사	I don't know how to stop playing the game.
명사절	that절	Columbus believed (that) the Earth is round.
	if/whether절	I wonder if[whether] she will come to the party.
	의문사절	I asked when he left.
	what절	Did he tell you what he would do?

3 주격 보어의 이해

주어를 설명해주는 주격 보어가 될 수 있는 것은 명사 상당어구, 형용사, 분사이다.

명사류		He is a professor. The problem is that we don't have enough time.
형용사류	형용사	He always looks neat.
	현재분사	She stayed smiling.
	과거분사	He remained unmarried all his life.

GRAMMAR POINT

수의 일치
- to부정사, 동명사, 절은 단수 취급한다.
  Memorizing lots of English words is very hard.
- 'the+형용사'는 복수 취급한다.

가주어-진주어 구문
- 길이가 긴 to부정사나 that절이 주어일 때, it을 가주어로 쓰고 to부정사나 that절은 뒤로 보낼 수 있다.
  It is easy to blame others.
  It is true that the pen is mightier than the sword.

목적어의 성격을 결정하는 동사
- to부정사만 목적어로 취하는 동사: want, wish, hope, expect, promise, decide
- 동명사만 목적어로 취하는 동사: mind, enjoy, give up, avoid, finish, escape
- 둘 다 목적어로 취하는 동사: like, hate, love, begin, start, continue

수식어구
- 명사는 전치사구 및 형용사절(관계사절)의 수식을 받을 수 있는데 이것도 문장 성분에 포함된다.
  The girl in the white dress is my sister.

형용사를 주격 보어로 취하는 동사
- be동사
- 상태 유지 동사: keep, stay, remain
- 상태 변화 동사: become, get, grow, turn(~되다)
- 감각 동사: look, sound, smell, taste, feel

현재분사와 과거분사
- 현재분사는 진행 및 능동의 의미를 나타내고, 과거분사는 수동 및 완료의 의미를 나타낸다.

VOCA blame 탓하다 | mobile 휴대폰 | app 앱 | convenient 편리한 | mightier 더 강한(mighty의 비교급) | sword 검, 칼 | admire 존경하다 | prevent 막다, 예방하다 | infectious 전염성의 | disease 병 | volunteer 자원봉사자 | unmarried 결혼하지 않은 | memorize 암기하다

A [ ]에서 알맞은 것을 고르시오. 각 1점

1 [Planning / Plan] for the future is important.

2 [Young / The young] aren't afraid of failure.

3 [When starting / When to start] is important in business.

4 [Whether he will come / He will come] is very important.

5 The teacher wants to know [what do I think / what I think].

6 [What I dream / That I dream] comes true.

B 밑줄 친 부분을 바르게 고쳐 쓰시오. 각 1점

1 I don't mind <u>help</u> you. → _____

2 I want <u>eat</u> fruits and vegetables. → _____

3 I think <u>what</u> he will accept the job. → _____

4 I am looking forward to <u>see</u> you. → _____

5 The bread feels <u>softly</u>. → _____

6 The young <u>has</u> lots of dreams. → _____

7 She remained <u>health</u> all her life. → _____

C 우리말 뜻과 일치하도록 주어진 단어를 배열하여 문장을 완성하시오. 각 1점

1 우리가 만난 그 남자는 영화배우였다. (whom, man, we, the, met)

→ _____ was a movie star.

2 네가 거리에서 주운 것이 그가 찾던 것이다. (picked, you, what, up)

→ _____ on the street is what he was looking for.

3 나는 그녀가 거짓말을 하지 않았다고 생각했다. (that, tell a lie, she, didn't)

→ I thought _____.

4 그녀는 훨씬 더 자신감 있어졌다. (more, much, confident)

→ She became _____.

5 무엇을 선택해야 하는지 내가 말했나? (to, what, select)

→ Did I mention _____?

VOCA plan 계획하다 | be afraid of ~을 두려워하다 | failure 실패 | vegetable 야채 | accept 받아들이다 | look forward to ~을 손꼽아 기다리다 | pick up 줍다 | tell a lie 거짓말을 하다 | confident 자신감 있는 | mention 언급하다, 말하다 | select 선택하다

Ready for Exams

》》 정답 2쪽

1 빈칸에 들어갈 수 있는 말이 <u>아닌</u> 것은? 2점

> _____ is important.

① You do your best

② Trying many things

③ Happiness

④ What to do

⑤ Whether he loves you or not

2 Which sentences are grammatically <u>incorrect</u>? 3점

> ⓐ Do you think what he is a smart man?
> ⓑ I asked him where he was going.
> ⓒ She remained silently during the meeting.
> ⓓ This is what I want.

① ⓐ, ⓑ   ② ⓐ, ⓑ, ⓒ   ③ ⓐ, ⓒ

④ ⓑ, ⓓ   ⑤ ⓓ

3 그림에 알맞은 문장을 조건에 맞게 완성하시오. 3점

> · 조건 1   어휘 – surround, small, people, by
> · 조건 2   위의 4단어만을 사용하되 필요한 경우에는 형태를 변형시킬 것

→ Gulliver lay _____.

4 Translate the sentence according to the conditions. 4점

> 그가 그 경기를 이길 것은 확실하다.
> · 조건 1   어휘 – the game, he, will, that, win, certain
> · 조건 2   위의 단어들을 포함하여 9단어로 쓸 것

→ _____

VOCA   surround 둘러싸다 | certain 확실한

14

02 목적격 보어

1 5형식 문장의 목적격 보어

「주어＋동사＋목적어＋목적격 보어」의 5형식 문장에서는 동사가 목적격 보어의 성격을 결정한다. 목적격 보어가 될 수 있는 것은 명사 상당어구, 형용사, 분사, 동사원형, to부정사이다.

A 목적격 보어가 명사인 경우

> make, consider, elect, name, call＋목적어＋목적격 보어(명사)

We elected him mayor.

B 목적격 보어가 형용사나 분사인 경우

> make, keep, leave, find＋목적어＋목적격 보어(형용사/분사)

The music made me happy.

My brother kept the door closed.

> 지각동사＋목적어＋현재분사
> 능동 관계

I saw the thief running. (능동. 진행 관계)

> 지각/사역동사＋목적어＋과거분사
> 수동 관계

I had my computer repaired. (수동 관계)

C 목적격 보어가 동사원형, to부정사인 경우

> 사역동사(make, have, let)＋목적어＋목적격 보어(동사원형)
> 지각동사(see, watch, hear, smell, feel)＋목적어＋목적격 보어(동사원형)

The doctor's smile made me feel at ease.

I saw him study late in his room.

> 준사역동사(help)＋목적어＋목적격 보어(동사원형/to부정사)
> 준사역동사(get)＋목적어＋목적격 보어(to부정사)

He helped me (to) complete my assignment.

My mom got me to clean the room.

> ask, tell, order, advise, want＋목적어＋목적격 보어(to부정사)

I don't want him to quit his job.

GRAMMAR POINT

목적격 보어란?
- 목적격 보어는 목적어를 보충 설명하는 말이다.

현재분사와 과거분사
- 목적어와 목적격 보어의 관계가 능동이면 현재분사, 수동이면 과거분사가 온다.

  We found him sleeping on the tree.
  (그가 자고 있는 능동 관계: 현재분사)

  I found my car stolen by the thief.
  (나의 차가 도난당한 수동 관계: 과거분사)

사역동사
- 사역동사는 make(만들다) ＞ have(시키다) ＞ let(허락하다)으로 강도의 차이가 있지만 주로 '～시키다'라는 의미의 동사류이다.
- get(시키다)동사도 목적격 보어로 to부정사를 취하는 준사역동사로 본다.

  He made me study.
  → He got me to study.

make 동사의 다양한 쓰임
- 3형식

  He made a robot.
  (그는 로봇을 만들었다.)

- 4형식

  He made me a robot.
  (그는 나에게 로봇을 만들어주었다.)

- 5형식

  He made me happy.
  (그는 나를 행복하게 만들었다.)

  He made me smile.
  (그는 나를 미소 짓게 만들었다.)

  The famous church made the town flooded with tourists.
  (그 유명한 교회는 그 마을을 관광객들로 넘쳐나게 만들었다.)

VOCA　elect 선출하다 | mayor 시장 | feel at ease 마음이 편안하다 | complete 끝마치다 | assignment 과제 | flood 넘치게 하다 | tourist 관광객

A 다음 [ ]에서 알맞은 것을 고르시오. 각 1점

1 They named the ship [the *Queen Mary* / as the *Queen Mary*].

2 We elected [she / her] chairman of our club.

3 I want you [be / to be] a world leader.

4 I heard the baby [to cry / cry] loudly.

5 I had my suitcase [carry / carried] to my room by a bellboy.

6 We heard the birds [sang / singing] in the tree.

B 밑줄 친 부분을 바르게 고쳐 쓰시오. 각 1점

1 That kind of movie always makes me <u>sadly</u>. → _____

2 Did you see the dog <u>to run</u> down the street? → _____

3 They asked me <u>talk</u> about my daily life. → _____

4 Suddenly, I heard my name <u>call</u>. → _____

5 BTS helped us <u>loving</u> ourselves through their → _____
   music.

C 우리말과 일치하도록 주어진 단어를 배열하시오. 각 1점

1 그는 우리가 6시에 일어나도록 만들었다. (get up, at 6 o'clock, made, us)

   → He _____.

2 누가 그녀를 파티에 오라고 했니? (the party, to, her, to, come, asked)

   → Who _____?

3 그는 내가 에세이 쓰는 것을 도와주지 않았다. (me, help, my essay, write)

   → He didn't _____.

4 나는 그 컵을 깨진 채로 두었다. (broken, the cup)

   → I left _____.

5 담임 선생님께서 우리에게 정각에 온라인 수업에 출석하라고 말씀하셨다.

   (to, us, on time, online classes, told, be, for)

   → My homeroom teacher _____.

VOCA name A B A를 B라고 부르다 | chairman 회장 | suitcase 여행 가방 | bellboy 벨보이(호텔에서 손님의 짐을 운반하는 사람) | daily life 일상생활 |
suddenly 갑자기 | essay 과제물(에세이, 리포트) | on time 정각에

16

Ready for Exams

>>> 정답 2쪽

My score is

Let's Check It Out _____ / 16점   0~20점 → Level 1 Test
Ready for Exams _____ / 14점   ⇒ 21~25점 → Level 2 Test
Total _____ / 30점   26~30점 → Level 3 Test

1   빈칸에 들어갈 알맞은 말을 고르시오. 2점

> Dad made me _____ to school instead of taking the bus.

① walk   ② to walk   ③ walked

④ walking   ⑤ walks

2   빈칸에 들어갈 말이 순서대로 짝지어진 것은? 3점

> • He has often seen his father _____ shoes.
> • Music can help us _____ better.
> • Let me _____ goodbye to him.

① to make – to concentrate – to say

② make – concentrating – say

③ making – concentrate – say

④ to make – concentrating – saying

⑤ make – to concentrate – to say

3   Rearrange the given words to make a complete sentence. 4점

> can, stay, exercise, you, help, healthy

→ _____

4   Look at the picture and complete the sentence by using the given words. 5점

> the general, the soldier, ordered, run

→ _____

VOCA   instead of ~ 대신에 | concentrate 집중하다 | general 장군 | soldier 군인 | order 명령하다

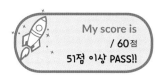

01 [보기]와 같은 의미의 문장을 <u>모두</u> 고르시오. 2점

> 보기 To get up early is difficult.

① It is difficult to get up early.
② That is difficult to get up early.
③ It is difficult that get up early.
④ What is difficult to get up early.
⑤ Getting up early is difficult.

02 Choose TWO correct translations of the given sentence. 3점

> 가난한 사람들이 평범한 사람들에게 도움을 받았다.

① The poor were helped by the ordinary.
② The poor was helped by the ordinary.
③ Poor people were helped by ordinary people.
④ Being poor were helped by being ordinary.
⑤ The poor were helped by ordinary.

03 다음 문장을 올바르게 설명한 것을 <u>모두</u> 고르시오. 2점

> The kid who is his son have musical talent.

① is는 are가 되어야 한다.
② have는 has가 되어야 한다.
③ who는 생략할 수 있다.
④ The kid가 음악적 재능을 가지고 있는 것이다.
⑤ The kid가 그의 아들이다.

04 다음 중 어법상 <u>어색한</u> 문장을 고르시오. 3점

① We do is more valuable than what we think.
② The questions on the test seem difficult.
③ What you said the other day was right.
④ They will give up searching for the man.
⑤ The teacher felt sad about the news.

05 빈칸에 들어갈 수 없는 것은? 2점

> Teddy made _____.

① you a toy   ② pizza
③ me shy   ④ her a princess
⑤ Suji to dance

06 Which of the following is NOT proper for the blank? 3점

> She _____ him to enjoy the concert.

① helped   ② saw
③ expected   ④ wanted
⑤ told

07 다음 중 어법상 <u>어색한</u> 문장을 고르시오. 3점

① My aunt encouraged me to start a blog.
② Jack helped me climbing up a tree.
③ Ms. Kim asked us to help her.
④ We made her open the door.
⑤ I saw some students bothering your sister.

08 Which sentences are grammatically <u>incorrect</u>? 4점

> ⓐ She got me sit on the floor.
> ⓑ He allowed us to join the club.
> ⓒ Did you see your brother fighting with someone?
> ⓓ It is good to see someone to keep the rules.
> ⓔ The rain made my clothes dirty.

① ⓐ   ② ⓐ, ⓓ
③ ⓑ, ⓓ   ④ ⓒ, ⓔ
⑤ ⓔ

09 U01_1
Rewrite the sentence correctly. 4점

> True doesn't ever change.
>
> ·조건 1   한 단어만 변형 가능
> ·조건 2   4단어로 쓸 것

→ _____

10 U01_1
우리말과 같은 의미가 되도록 문장을 바르게 고쳐 다시 쓰시오. 5점

> 우리가 알고 있는 것이 전부가 아니다.
> = We know is not everything.

→ _____

11 U01_2+GP
다음은 여행 광고문이다. 어법상 어색한 부분을 찾아 고치시오. (단, 그림에 나온 단어만을 사용할 것) 5점
함정

_____ → _____

12 U01_3
우리말과 일치하도록 주어진 단어를 사용하여 문장을 완성하시오. 4점

> 우리는 헤어진 후에 친구로 남았다. (remain)

→ We _____ _____ after our
breakup.

13 U01_GP
Look at the picture and translate the sentence by rearranging the given words. 4점

> 교실에 있는 그 책상은 유리로 만들어졌다.
> the classroom, the desk, made, in, is, of, glass

→ _____

14 U02_1C
우리말과 일치하도록 주어진 단어를 배열하여 문장을 완성하시오. 4점

> 그는 나에게 숙제를 도와달라고 부탁했다.
> homework, with, help, to, him, his, asked, me

→ He _____

15 U02_1B
Translate the sentence according to the conditions. 7점
★ 고난도

> 너는 언제 너희 집을 리모델링 받았니?
>
> ·조건 1   어휘 – have, house, remodel을 활용할 것
> ·조건 2   7단어로 쓸 것

→ _____

16 U02_1B
[보기]와 같이 주어진 문장을 다시 쓰시오 5점

> 보기 She was studying in the library.
>   → He found her studying in the library.
>
> She was crying in her room.

→ He found _____

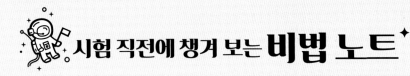

한눈에 쏙! 아래 노트를 보면서 빈칸을 채워 보세요.

1 주격 보어

주어 + 동사 + 주격 보어

→ 명사류

→ 명사류/형용사/분사(-ing, p.p.)

2 목적격 보어

주어 + 동사 + 목적어 + 목적격 보어

→ 명사류

→ 명사류

→ 명사류/형용사/동사류

① 사역동사(make, ¹⁾h_ _ _ _, ²⁾_ _ _ _)	동사원형
② 지각동사(³⁾s_ _ _, ⁴⁾w_ _ _ _ _, ⁵⁾h_ _ _ _, ⁶⁾sm_ _ _ _, ⁷⁾f_ _ _ _)	
③ 준사역동사(⁸⁾h_ _ _ _)	(to) 동사원형
④ ask, tell, order, advise, want	to+동사원형(= to부정사)

헷갈리지 말자! 초록색으로 표시된 부분을 바르게 고쳐 쓰세요.

1 Listening to good music makes me happily.

2 My mom let me to sleep after finishing my homework.

3 Facebook messenger helps us contacted each other regularly.

4 The government asked people wear a mask.

20

CHAPTER 02
to부정사

UNIT 03   **용법, 의미상의 주어, 부정**

UNIT 04   **시제, 독립부정사, 대부정사**

UNIT 03 용법, 의미상의 주어, 부정

CONCEPT 1 to부정사의 용법

A 명사적 용법

주어 역할	To hide our true feelings is not easy.
목적어 역할	When do you expect to see him back?
보어 역할	My mom's dream was to be a firefighter.

B 형용사적 용법

명사 수식	They need a smart leader to lead their team.
대명사 수식	My sister has been looking for somebody to marry.

C 부사적 용법

목적	I drink coffee (in order[so as]) to keep awake.
감정의 원인	The hacker was pleased to figure out the password.
판단의 근거	He must be foolish to buy the used phone.
결과	The witch lived to be 999 years old.
형용사 수식	The machine is complicated to use.

가주어-진주어 구문
- to부정사가 주어인 경우는 주로 가주어−진주어(It ~ to...) 구문으로 쓴다.

  It is important to work out regularly.

  (규칙적으로 운동하는 것은 중요하다.)

to부정사 + 전치사
- 수식받는 말이 전치사의 목적어일 경우 전치사를 꼭 표시해야 한다.

  The girl wanted to have a friend to talk with.

  (그 소녀는 함께 이야기할 친구를 갖고 싶어 했다.)

CONCEPT 2 to부정사의 의미상의 주어

to부정사의 행위의 주체를 말하며 'for/of+목적격'으로 쓴다.

일반 형용사	easy, difficult, hard, necessary, possible, impossible, interesting, important	for+목적격
성품 형용사	kind, nice, foolish, stupid, polite, rude, careful, careless, brave, wise, silly, mean	of+목적격

The camel is dangerous for you to ride on.

Was it silly of me to expect you to help me?

CONCEPT 3 to부정사의 부정

to부정사의 부정은 to 앞에 not 또는 never를 쓴다.

> not[never] to+동사원형

I left early not to miss the train for Jeongdongjin.

She promised never to leave me alone.

to부정사의 주체를 표현하지 않는 경우
- 주체가 주어인 경우

  He decided to lose 6kg this month.

  (to lose의 주체가 주어인 He)

- 주체가 목적어인 경우

  My mom wants me to go to Canada.

  (to go의 주체가 목적어인 me)

- 주체가 일반인인 경우

  It is necessary to follow the traffic rules.

  (to follow의 주체가 일반인)

to부정사의 부정과 동사의 부정
- She didn't tell me to text at midnight. (tell을 부정)

- She told me not to text at midnight. (text를 부정)

VOCA expect 기대하다 | hacker 해커 | pleased 기쁜 | figure out ~을 알아내다 | witch 마녀 | complicated 복잡한 | camel 낙타 | regularly 규칙적으로 | midnight 자정

22

Let's Check It Out

>>> 정답 3쪽

My score is

/ 17점

A 밑줄 친 to부정사의 용법을 쓰시오. 각 1점

1 The kid grew up <u>to be</u> a pro gamer.　　➡ _____

2 It is fun <u>to make</u> a paper swan.　　➡ _____

3 The frog needed someone <u>to kiss</u> him.　　➡ _____

4 Her mother felt sorry <u>to hear</u> that.　　➡ _____

B 밑줄 친 부분에서 어색한 것을 바르게 고치시오. 각 1점

1 Was it <u>easy of you to find</u> this place?

   _____ ➡ _____

2 How <u>kind for her to help</u> the old man!

   _____ ➡ _____

3 It was <u>difficult for we to prepare</u> for the festival.

   _____ ➡ _____

4 It was <u>brave for the children to save</u> the dog.

   _____ ➡ _____

C 주어진 단어를 이용하여 문장을 완성하시오. 각 1점

1 I decided _____ _____ _____ her a secret again.
   (never, tell)

2 We all did our best _____ _____ _____ at tug-of-war.
   (not, lose)

3 He promised _____ _____ _____ the class. (not, skip)

4 I quietly went out of the room _____ _____ _____
   _____ the baby. (not, wake up)

D 주어진 단어를 바르게 배열하여 빈칸에 쓰시오. 각 1점

1 The lake is _____. (swim, in, dangerous, to)

2 He walked about _____ warm. (to, keep, order, in)

3 Is it _____ jump over the wall? (to, me, for, possible)

4 It's not _____ all his money. (of, spend, to, him, wise)

5 The lady told me _____ about the rumor. (worry,
   not, to)

VOCA　paper swan 종이 학 | prepare 준비하다 | festival 축제 | tug-of-war 줄다리기 | skip 거르다, 빠지다 | rumor 소문

My score is

Let's Check It Out _____ / 17점   0~20점 → Level 1 Test
Ready for Exams _____ / 13점 ➡ 21~25점 → Level 2 Test
Total _____ / 30점   26~30점 → Level 3 Test

>>> 정답 3쪽

1   Which is NOT suitable for the blank? 2점

| It was _____ of her to do the task alone. |

① silly   ② wise   ③ necessary

④ careless   ⑤ smart

2   밑줄 친 부분의 쓰임이 [보기]와 같은 것의 개수는? 2점

> 보기   Are you really going to university <u>to study</u> law?
>
> ⓐ I was delighted <u>to find</u> my puppy.
> ⓑ He must have a cold <u>to be coughing</u> so often.
> ⓒ She pretended not <u>to see</u> me coming.
> ⓓ This grammar book is surely fun <u>to study</u>.
> ⓔ It isn't easy <u>to pronounce</u> the word correctly.

① 0개   ② 1개   ③ 2개

④ 3개   ⑤ 4개

3   다음 그림을 보고 오늘의 영어 한마디를 완성하시오. 4점

내가 다섯 아이들을 키우는 것은 식은 죽 먹기죠.

· 표현   a piece of cake: 식은 죽 먹기
        raise: 키우다

→ It is _____ five kids.

4   Translate the sentence according to the conditions. 5점

> 난 그 남자에게 다시 나에게 전화하지 말라고 말할 거야.
>
> · 조건 1   8번째 단어는 3글자로 쓸 것
> · 조건 2   어휘 – be going to, tell, the guy, call
> · 조건 3   주어진 어휘를 포함하여 12단어로 쓸 것

→ _____

VOCA   task 업무 | delighted 기쁜 | cough 기침하다 | pretend ~인 체하다 | pronounce 발음하다

24

UNIT 04 시제, 독립부정사, 대부정사

CONCEPT 1 부정사의 시제

종류	형태	의미
단순부정사	to+동사원형	본동사와 같거나 앞으로 다가올 시제
완료부정사	to have+p.p.	본동사보다 먼저 일어난 이전 시제

She seems to be interested in physics. (같은 시제)

→ It seems that she is interested in physics.

He promised to treat me to dinner tonight. (앞으로 다가올 시제)

→ He promised that he would treat me to dinner tonight.

They appear to have made a big mistake. (먼저 일어난 이전 시제)

→ It appears that they made a big mistake.

GRAMMAR POINT

본동사가 과거일 때 완료부정사의 의미

- She seemed <u>to have eaten</u> lunch already.
  → It seemed that she had eaten lunch already.

부정문의 경우

- The marathoner doesn't seem to run hard.
  → It doesn't seem that the marathoner runs hard.

CONCEPT 2 독립부정사

to부정사가 독립적으로 사용되면서 문장 전체를 수식하는 것을 말한다.

to be sure (확실히)	She will, to be sure, come back soon.
to begin with (우선)	To begin with, I'd like to thank all of you.
to tell (you) the truth (사실을 말하자면)	To tell the truth, he didn't attend Harvard.
to be honest[frank] (with you) (솔직히 말하면)	To be honest, I don't know what it means.
to be brief (간단히 말하면)	To be brief, we need to accept her offer.
to make matters[things] worse (설상가상으로)	To make matters worse, I've lost my wallet.
sad to say (슬픈 이야기지만)	Sad to say, the lost dog was never found.
strange to say (이상한 말이지만)	Strange to say, I didn't like Christmas when I was little.
so to speak (말하자면)	Now he is, so to speak, a mouse in a trap.
not to mention (= needless to say) (~은 말할 것도 없이)	The chef has a big restaurant here, not to mention a steakhouse in Miami.

CONCEPT 3 대부정사

동사의 중복을 피하기 위해 'to+동사원형'에서 동사를 생략하고 to만 쓰는 형태를 말한다.

~ to (반복어구 생략)

A: Would you like to have a caramel macchiato?

B: Yes, I'd love to (have a caramel macchiato).

VOCA physics 물리학 | treat 한 턱 내다 | marathoner 마라톤 선수 | attend 다니다 | accept 받아들이다 | offer 제안

>>> 정답 3쪽

A 다음과 같이 문장 전환을 할 때 빈칸에 알맞은 말을 쓰시오. 각 1점

1 She seems to be happy.

→ It _____ that she _____ happy.

2 Ted seemed to work hard.

→ It _____ that Ted _____ hard.

3 It seems that your daughter is sick.

→ Your daughter _____ _____ _____ sick.

4 It appeared that the pirates had attacked the ship.

→ The pirates _____ ____ ____ _____ _____ the ship.

5 It didn't seem that he had lost a significant amount of blood.

→ He _____ _____ _____ _____ _____ a significant amount of blood.

B 우리말과 일치하도록 빈칸을 채우시오. 각 1점

1 확실히, 그의 아버지는 아주 성공한 사업가였다.

→ _____, his father was a very successful businessman.

2 사실을 말하자면, 내가 그 답을 알고 있는지 잘 모르겠어.

→ _____, I'm not sure I know the answer.

3 솔직히 말해, 그녀는 널 전혀 사랑하지 않았어.

→ _____, she didn't love you at all.

4 슬픈 이야기지만, 쉽게 번 돈은 부를 만들지 않아.

→ _____, easy money doesn't create wealth.

5 우선, 너는 입을 다물고 있는 게 낫겠다.

→ _____, you'd better keep your mouth shut.

C 생략 가능한 부분에 밑줄을 치시오. 각 1점

1 You can stay here if you want to stay here.

2 I can help her, but she never asks me to help her.

3 A: Will you come to the party?

   B: Sure. I'd love to go to the party.

VOCA pirate 해적 | attack 공격하다 | significant 상당한 | amount 양 | successful 성공한 | businessman 사업가 | create 만들다 | wealth 부

1 다음 중 문장 전환을 바르게 하지 <u>못한</u> 학생은? 2점

① 지현: Hyeona seems to be nice.
→ It seems that Hyeona is nice.

② 현아: Ayoung seems to be right.
→ It seems that Ayoung is right.

③ 아영: Youngmi seemed to copy my homework.
→ It seemed that Youngmi copies my homework.

④ 영미: Miyeon seemed to like me.
→ It seemed that Miyeon liked me.

⑤ 미연: Jihyeon seemed to have met my boyfriend.
→ It seemed that Jihyeon had met my boyfriend.

2 다음 문장에서 어법상 <u>어색한</u> 부분을 찾아 바르게 고친 것은? 2점

> Strangely to say, it hasn't snowed all winter.

① Strangely → Strange
② to say → saying
③ it → the weather
④ hasn't → haven't
⑤ snowed → snowing

3 다음 문장을 조건에 맞게 영작하시오. 4점

> 네가 원한다면 내 차를 운전해도 좋아.
> - 조건 1 6번째 단어는 if를 쓸 것
> - 조건 2 어휘 – want
> - 조건 3 주어진 어휘를 포함하여 9단어로 쓸 것

→ _____

4 우리말과 같은 뜻이 되도록 주어진 단어 카드를 바르게 배열하여 문장을 완성하시오. 4점

> 네가 원할 때면 언제든지 널 도와줄게.
>
> | you | you | to | want | help | whenever | me |

→ I will _____ .

VOCA copy 베끼다 ∣ whenever 언제든지

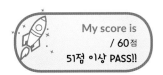

>>> 정답 4쪽

---

01 U03_1

밑줄 친 부분의 쓰임이 [보기]와 다른 것을 고르시오. 2점

> 보기 It is fun to go to an amusement park.

① To borrow money from her is impossible.
② My duty is to protect the singer.
③ He looked away to avoid talking with her.
④ It is his dream to live a rewarding life.
⑤ We agreed to stop the debate for a while.

---

02 U03_2

Which is NOT proper for the blank? 2점

> It was _____ for me to take the Russian language course.

① easy   ② difficult
③ necessary   ④ silly
⑤ important

---

03 U03_3

함정

다음을 영작할 때 3번째 올 단어는? 3점

> 감기 걸리지 않게 조심해라.

① to   ② don't
③ not   ④ catch
⑤ a

---

04 U04_1

한눈에 쏙

다음 문장을 바르게 이해한 학생은? (답 2개) 3점

> Carmen seems to lose interest in studying.
> Her grades have gotten worse.

① 유나: 관심을 잃은 것이므로 lost로 써야 해.
② 규리: 내용상 관심을 잃은 것이 앞선 일이니까 완료부정사로 써야 해.
③ 정민: 주절의 시제가 seems로 현재니까 'to+동사원형'이 맞아.
④ 가연: It seems that Carmen lost interest in studying.으로 바꿔 쓸 수 있어.
⑤ 현아: 과거 시제로 Carmen seemed to lose interest in studying.으로 써야 해.

---

05 U04_1

She를 주어로 해서 다음 문장을 전환할 때 필요한 단어 3개는? 2점

> It appears that she was a doctor.

① appeared   ② to
③ be   ④ have
⑤ been

---

06 U04_2

밑줄 친 우리말에 해당하는 표현을 고르시오. 2점

> 솔직히 말해서, I don't think it was my fault.

① To begin with
② Strange to say
③ So to speak
④ Needless to say
⑤ To be frank

---

07 U03_1+3+U04_3

Which words are correct for the blanks? 2점

> He decided _____ alone, but I told him
> _____.

① going – to
② going – not to
③ to go – not to
④ to go – to
⑤ to go – not going

---

08 U03_3+U04_1

고난도

다음 중 어법상 어색한 문장의 개수는? 4점

> ⓐ She seemed that she was tired.
> ⓑ Please tell him not visit my house.
> ⓒ It is polite of her to show them the way.
> ⓓ I will give them a lesson if you want me to.
> ⓔ It must be terrible to be poor and hungry.

① 1개   ② 2개
③ 3개   ④ 4개
⑤ 5개

09 U03_1C

한눈에 쏙

Translate the sentence by rearranging the given words. 5점

> 그는 돌아와서 자신의 딸이 병상에 누운 것을 발견했다.
> find, daughter, to, came, he, back, sick in bed, his

→ _____

_____

10 U03_2

고난도

다음 중 어법상 어색한 것을 찾아 바르게 고치시오. 5점

> ⓐ Isn't it selfish for her to eat the cake all by herself?
> ⓑ In the past, it was impossible for black people to sit in certain seats.

(　　) _____ → _____

11 U03_3+U04_3

고난도

Among the underlined parts, find TWO errors and correct them 6점

> My sister plays loud music in the ⓐ living room at night. It makes me really mad. I asked her ⓑ not play music at night, but she didn't listen ⓒ to. I don't know ⓓ what to do.

(　　) → _____

(　　) → _____

12 U03_2

함정

Choose the necessary words and rearrange them to describe the picture. 5점

> him, he, was, for, to, touch, of, it, careless

→ _____

the plug with wet hands.

13 U04_1

함정

다음 두 문장을 It seems/seemed that ~ 구문으로 전환하시오. 5점

(1) She seems to be diligent.

→ _____

(2) She seemed to be diligent.

→ _____

14 U04_3

다음 대화의 밑줄 친 to 다음에 생략된 말을 쓰시오. 4점

> A: Hey! You stepped on my foot!
> B: Oh, I'm sorry. I didn't mean to.

→ _____ .

15 U04_2

밑줄 친 우리말 표현을 조건에 맞게 영어로 쓰시오. 4점

> I was in a hurry, and, 설상가상으로, the car broke down.
> ·조건 1 to부정사를 쓸 것
> ·조건 2 4단어로 쓸 것

→ _____

16 U03_3

다음은 엄마가 아들에게 남겨놓은 쪽지이다. [보기]와 같이 문장을 바꿔 쓰시오. 각 3점

> 보기 Do your homework first.
> → Mom told me to do my homework first.

(1) Do not make a mess.

→ Mom told me _____ .

(2) Never turn on the computer.

→ Mom told me _____ .

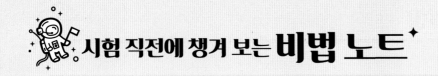

>>> 정답 4쪽

한눈에 쏙! 아래 노트를 보면서 빈칸을 채워 보세요.

1 to부정사의 용법

① 명사적 용법	주어, 1)목＿＿, 2)＿＿ 역할
② 3)＿＿＿＿ 용법	명사 수식, 대명사 수식
③ 부사적 용법	(목적) 감정의 4)＿＿, 판단의 5)＿＿, 6)＿＿, 형용사 수식

2 의미상의 주어

일반 형용사 → 1)＿＿＿ + 목적격   2)＿＿ + 형용사 → (of) + 목적격

3 to부정사의 시제

① to + 1)＿＿＿＿＿＿	본동사와 같거나 다가올 시제
② to + 2)＿＿＿ + 3)＿＿＿	본동사보다 앞선 시제

헷갈리지 말자! 초록색으로 표시된 부분을 바르게 고쳐 쓰세요.

1 Shinbi lived being 100 years old.

2 It was stupid for me to accept her proposal.

3 We came back early to not be late for school.

4 It seems that we made a big hit. = We seem to make a big hit.

5 He will, to be surely, leave the stage someday.

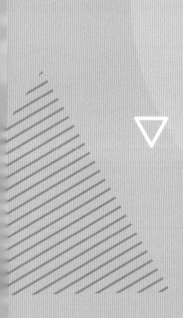

CHAPTER 03
동명사

UNIT 05   **용법, 의미상의 주어, 부정**
UNIT 06   **동명사, 현재분사, to부정사**

UNIT 05

용법, 의미상의 주어, 부정

1 동명사의 용법

동사에 -ing를 붙여 명사 역할을 하는 것을 말한다.

주어 역할	Taking pictures here is not allowed.
보어 역할	What I hate the most is repeating myself.
동사의 목적어 역할	My girlfriend likes going to the movies with me.
전치사의 목적어 역할	Can you sneeze without closing your eyes?

2 동명사의 의미상의 주어

동명사의 행위의 주체를 말하며 '소유격+-ing' 형태가 기본이다.

사람, 생물	소유격[목적격]+-ing
부정대명사, 무생물	목적격+-ing

Do you mind my[me] taking a bite of your cookie?

I appreciate your[you] helping me with the work.

I forgot somebody calling me last night.

He clearly remembered Liuliu saying that.

3 동명사의 부정

동명사의 부정은 동명사 앞에 not 또는 never를 쓴다.

not[never]+-ing

Thank you for not telling that to anybody.

The guide suggested never climbing the mountain alone.

GRAMMAR POINT

동명사의 수

• 동명사가 주어인 경우 단수 취급 한다.

Taking care of a pet requires patience.

의미상의 주어에서 목적격 사용

• 목적격은 동명사가 타동사나 전치사의 목적어인 경우에만 가능하다.

Him (→ His) attending the yoga class looks impossible. (주어)

• 형태는 소유격이어도 의미상의 주어이므로 '-이/-가'로 해석한다.

She is worried about his being sick.

(그녀는 그가 아픈 것에 대해 걱정한다.)

동명사의 주체를 표시하지 않는 경우

• 주체가 주어인 경우

My sister loves eating fried chicken.

(eating의 주체가 My sister)

• 주체가 목적어인 경우

Thank you for inviting me.

(inviting의 주체가 you)

• 주체가 일반인인 경우

Walking fast is good exercise.

(Walking의 주체가 일반인)

의미상의 주어와 동명사의 부정

• We can't imagine not his (→ his not) skipping the class.

본동사의 부정과 동명사의 부정

• I don't regret telling you the story.

(말한 것을 후회하지 않음)

• I regret not telling you the story.

(말하지 않은 것을 후회함)

VOCA allow 허락하다 | repeat oneself 같은 말을 되풀이하다 | sneeze 재채기 하다 | take a bite 한 입 먹다 | appreciate 고마워하다 | suggest 제안하다 | require 요구하다

>>> 정답 4쪽

A 밑줄 친 동명사의 역할을 구분하시오. ^{각 1점}

1 <u>Walking</u> is the easiest way to lose weight.   → _____

2 My ex-boyfriend left without <u>saying</u> anything.   → _____

3 Her hobby is <u>collecting</u> Barbie dolls.   → _____

4 They like <u>watching</u> movies at the movie theater.   → _____

5 Is <u>listening</u> to heavy metal your daughter's hobby?   → _____

B 괄호 안에 주어진 단어를 빈칸에 알맞은 형태로 쓰시오. ^{각 1점}

1 They insisted on _____ going there. (I)

2 He was afraid of _____ going away. (she)

3 There is no possibility of _____ winning the game. (he)

4 She dreamed of _____ falling down on her house. (the tree)

5 I don't like _____ telling me what to do. (you)

C 주어진 단어를 이용하여 문장을 완성하시오. ^{각 1점}

1 I am terribly sorry for _____ _____ on time. (not, be)

2 Mika imagined _____ _____ a test tomorrow. (not, have)

3 The secret to success is _____ _____ a lie. (never, tell)

D 우리말과 일치하도록 주어진 단어를 활용하여 빈칸을 채우시오. ^{각 1점}

1 Roger, 널 의심해서 미안해. (suspect)

→ I am _____, Roger, for _____ you.

2 내가 일찍 떠나는 것에 대해 화내지 말아요. (mad, leave)

→ Don't be _____ about _____ _____ early.

3 시작하기는 쉽지만, 계속하기는 어렵다. (begin, continue)

→ _____ is easy, but _____ is hard.

4 그 개구리는 엄마 말을 듣지 않았던 것을 후회하고 있다. (listen)

→ The frog regrets _____ _____ _____ his mom.

5 실패는 넘어지는 것이 아니라, 일어서려 하지 않는 것이다. (fall, refuse)

→ Failure is not _____ down but _____ to get up.

VOCA ex-boyfriend 전 남자친구 | insist 우기다 | possibility 가능성 | terribly 몹시 | suspect 의심하다 | regret 후회하다 | refuse ~하려 하지 않다, 거절하다

★ **Ready for Exams**

>>> 정답 5쪽

My score is

Let's Check It Out _____ / 18점   0~20점 → Level 1 Test
Ready for Exams _____ / 12점 ➡ 21~25점 → Level 2 Test
Total _____ / 30점   26~30점 → Level 3 Test

1 밑줄 친 부분의 역할이 주어진 문장과 같은 것은? 2점

His favorite activity is <u>fishing</u> with his grandpa.

① Were you afraid of <u>getting</u> the results?
② She gave up <u>taking</u> the philosophy course.
③ My brother's hobby is <u>playing</u> the drum.
④ <u>Learning</u> new things is always challenging.
⑤ The man avoided <u>answering</u> the officer's question.

2 Who analyzes the given sentences correctly? 3점

ⓐ His coming here was a kind of blessing.
ⓑ I am ashamed of not protecting our town.

① 수은: ⓐ His를 Him으로 써도 돼.
② 지민: ⓐ coming의 의미상의 주어는 His야.
③ 정민: ⓐ His는 소유격이니까 '그의'라고 해석해야 해.
④ 꽃별: ⓑ of 다음에는 동명사를 쓰니까 not을 지워야 해.
⑤ 헌정: ⓑ not protecting을 not to protect로 써야 해.

3 조건에 맞게 우리말을 영작하시오. 4점

학생들은 선생님이 잔소리하는 것을 싫어했다.

· 조건 1 문장의 주어와 동명사의 의미상의 주어에 정관사를 쓸 것
· 조건 2 어휘 – hate, nag(잔소리하다)

→ _____

4 Look at the picture and rearrange the given words. 3점

Oh, it's Monday again. Should I skip work today?

work, not, to, he, going, considering, is

→ _____.

VOCA result 결과 | philosophy 철학 | blessing 축복 | be ashamed of ~을 부끄럽게 생각하다 | skip work 일을 거르다 | consider 고려하다

UNIT 06 동명사, 현재분사, to부정사

CONCEPT 1 동명사와 현재분사

	동명사	현재분사
기능	명사(주어, 목적어, 보어)	형용사, 진행형
표현	용도, 목적	동작, 상태

She wants to buy a new sewing machine. (용도, 목적 → 동명사)

The little baby is swimming alone in the sea. (동작, 상태 → 현재분사)

I enjoy watching horror movies. (목적어 → 동명사)

She was reading a book about Japanese cuisine. (진행형 → 현재분사)

CONCEPT 2 동명사와 to부정사

동사	목적어
dislike, finish, enjoy, mind, give up, delay, avoid, deny, keep (on), postpone, put off, suggest, consider, practice	동명사
want, hope, wish, plan, agree, decide, choose, refuse, expect, would like, promise, fail	to부정사
like, love, hate, begin, start, continue	둘 다

She didn't mind looking after my 2-year-old girl.

He promised to buy the ring I wanted.

When we came out, it started raining[to rain].

CONCEPT 3 동명사의 관용적 표현

- on+-ing (~하자마자)
- go+-ing (~하러 가다)
- feel like+-ing (~하고 싶디)
- be far from+-ing (~하는 것과 거리가 멀다)
- be tired of+-ing (~에 싫증이 나다)
- How[What] about+-ing ~? (~하는 게 어때?)
- go on+-ing (= continue+-ing) (계속 ~하다)
- be used[accustomed] to+-ing (~하는 것에 익숙하다)
- spend[waste] 시간[돈]+-ing (~하느라 시간[돈]을 쓰다[낭비하다])
- have difficulty[trouble, a hard time]+-ing (~하는 데 어려움을 겪다)
- be worth+-ing (~할 가치가 있다)
- cannot help+-ing (~하지 않을 수 없다)
- be busy+-ing (~히느라 비쁘디)
- It's no use[good]+-ing (~해봐야 소용없다)
- look forward to+-ing (~하기를 고대하다)
- There is no+-ing (~하는 것은 불가능하다)

On seeing me, she turned around.

They went on running up and down the hill.

Are you still busy finishing the project?

His words are far from being true.

VOCA sew 바느질하다 | horror 공포 | cuisine 요리 | look after ~을 돌보다 | turn around 돌아서다 | project 과제

Let's Check It Out

>>> 정답 5쪽

A 동명사나 현재분사에 밑줄을 치고 둘 중 무엇인지 쓰시오. 각 1점

1 Are you fond of eating spinach? → _____

2 Is he talking about his lizards again? → _____

3 Haven't I told you to buy a walking stick? → _____

4 Who in the world is the girl waving at you? → _____

5 I woke up this morning and saw the rising sun. → _____

B 괄호 안의 단어를 빈칸에 알맞은 형태로 쓰시오. 각 1점

1 What did he suggest _____? (do)

2 He didn't expect _____ his teacher at the Internet café. (see)

3 The audience continued _____ for an encore. (shout)

4 What city would you like _____? (visit)

5 I forgot _____ the email yesterday, so I'm sending it now.
(send)

C 우리말과 일치하도록 주어진 단어를 활용하여 빈칸을 채우시오. 각 1점

1 넌 똑같은 종류의 치킨을 먹는 것이 지겹지 않니? (tired, eat)

→ _____ you _____ _____ _____ the same kind
of chicken?

2 난 네 생각을 하지 않을 수가 없었어. (can't, help)

→ I _____ _____ _____ about you.

3 주말 동안 차를 대여하는 게 어때? (how, rent)

→ _____ _____ _____ a car for the weekend?

4 Kate는 갑자기 고향으로 돌아가고 싶었다. (feel, go back)

→ Kate suddenly _____ _____ _____ _____ to
her hometown.

D [ ]에서 알맞은 것을 고르시오. 각 1점

1 I would like [living / to live] forever.

2 Stop [wishing / to wish]! Start doing!

3 Why do you dislike [being / to be] with people?

4 She remembered [to see / seeing] him when she was a kid.

VOCA　be fond of ~을 좋아하다 | spinach 시금치 | lizard 도마뱀 | walking stick 지팡이 | wave 손을 흔들다 | suggest 제안하다 | audience 관중 |
encore 앙코르

36

My score is

Let's Check It Out _____ / 18점   0~20점 → Level 1 Test
Ready for Exams _____ / 12점   ➡ 21~25점 → Level 2 Test
Total _____ / 30점   26~30점 → Level 3 Test

1 밑줄 친 단어가 동명사인 문장을 모두 고른 학생은? 3점

> ⓐ Can you put me on the <u>waiting</u> list?
> ⓑ The man <u>playing</u> basketball alone is my uncle.
> ⓒ Your kid was <u>enjoying</u> the party.
> ⓓ I'm thinking of <u>moving</u> to another city.

① 현지: ⓐ   ② 수민: ⓑ, ⓒ   ③ 승은: ⓐ, ⓓ
④ 민규: ⓐ, ⓑ, ⓒ   ⑤ 동민: ⓐ, ⓑ, ⓒ, ⓓ

2 Which is grammatically <u>incorrect</u>? 2점

① Did you enjoy skiing during the winter?
② He stopped asking me to join the club.
③ She finally gave up to play computer games.
④ His father wants to stop drinking.
⑤ I tried to protect myself from the wind.

3 Find the error and correct it. 3점

> I remember to enjoy a meal at the Italian restaurant about three years ago.

_____ ➡ _____

4 다음은 연극의 한 장면이다. 밑줄 친 우리말을 조건에 맞게 영작하시오. 4점

Villain: <u>도와달라고 울어봐야 소용없단다.</u>
          No one will hear you. Ha-ha-ha!
Kevin: My father will come to save me!
                                    *villain: 악당

· 조건   use가 들어가는 동명사의 관용 표현을 이용해
         서 7단어로 쓸 것
· 힌트   cry for help: 도와달라고 울다

➡ _____

VOCA   join 가입하다 | protect 보호하다 | save 구하다

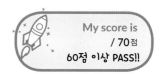
>>> 정답 5쪽

U05_1+U06_2

01 빈칸에 들어갈 말이 바르게 짝지어진 것은? 2점

> The man kept on _____ without _____ attention to the noise.

① working – paying
② worked – paid
③ to work – to pay
④ work – pay
⑤ to work – not paying

U05_1+2

02 다음 문장에서 어법상 어색한 부분을 찾아 바르게 고친 것은? (답 2개) 3점

> We are very sorry about he having an accident.

① he → him   ② having → have
③ an → a   ④ he → his
⑤ having → to have

U05_1+U06_2

03 Which is grammatically correct? 4점

★ 고난도

① Teaching playful children are not my thing.
② Loving other people mean accepting others.
③ Would you mind to closing the door for me?
④ She has been interested in help others.
⑤ I study English hard to get good grades.

U06_GP

04 Which is proper for the blank? 2점

> She forgot _____ me about the meeting, so I didn't know about it at all.

① email
② to email
③ emailing
④ to have emailed
⑤ having emailed

U06_1

05 밑줄 친 말의 쓰임이 나머지 넷과 다른 것은? 3점

① I was <u>watching</u> a movie at that time.
② My grandpa doesn't need a <u>walking</u> stick.
③ Did you see the <u>singing</u> boys on the way here?
④ The man <u>standing</u> there is my cousin from Uzbekistan.
⑤ Your brother was <u>reading</u> a car magazine.

U06_3

06 주어진 단어들을 조합하여 올바른 문장을 만들 수 없는 것은? 4점

★ 고난도

① inviting / no / there / is / Rocky / .
② talking / is / phone / . / on / the / busy / Clare
③ mirrors / . / spent / all / Rachel / her / money / on
④ not / Jenna / is / spicy / ramen / . / to / eating / used
⑤ forward / married / . / to / Zinna / looking / get / is

U05_1+3+U06_3

07 다음 중 어법상 어색한 것은? (답 2개) 4점

★ 고난도

① I'm sorry for not go to your party.
② Listening to their music makes me so bored.
③ We wasted an hour to wait for him.
④ His hobby is taking pictures of wildflowers.
⑤ Thanks for being with us on our trip.

U06_2

08 How many words are NOT proper for the blank? 3점

함정

> Mr. McGuire _____ drawing a picture of a turkey.
>
> | ⓐ enjoyed | ⓑ finished | ⓒ began |
> | ⓓ wanted | ⓔ stopped | ⓕ promised |

① 1개   ② 2개
③ 3개   ④ 4개
⑤ 5개

U05_1+3

09 Rewrite the sentence by correcting the errors. 4점

The secretary's mistake was lock not the door.

→ _____

_____

U05_1

10 두 문장의 뜻이 같도록 빈칸에 알맞은 말을 쓰시오. 4점

He is proud of the fact that he is from Kenya.

→ He is proud of _____ _____

_____.

U04_1+U05_2

11 Look at the picture and fill in the blanks to translate the sentence. 4점

민준(Minjun)이가 경주에서 이길 가능성은 없어 보인다.

→ There seems to _____

_____ the race.

U05_2+3

12 괄호 안의 어휘를 빈칸에 알맞게 배열하시오. 6점

★ 고난도

He punished (on, not, her, arriving, for, time).

→ He punished _____.

U06_2

13 다음 두 문장 중 어색한 것을 찾아 바르게 고치시오. 5점

◉ 한눈에 쏙

ⓐ It began to rain heavily in the morning.
ⓑ Ashley disliked to sing with me at the party.

( ) _____ → _____

U06_1+U05_1

14 그림을 보고, 빈칸에 공통으로 들어갈 말을 쓰고, 동명사인지 현재분사인지 구분하시오. 각 3점

(1) Look at the _____ girl.

→ _____

(2) It seems that _____ is her favorite thing.

→ _____

U06_3

15 우리말과 일치하도록 주어진 단어를 사용하고, 필요한 단어를 보충하여 영작을 완성하시오. 5점

우리는 다시 숲으로 돌아가고 싶었다.
feel, go, back, the

→ _____

U06_2_GP

16 우리말과 일치하도록 주어진 단어 중에서 필요한 것만 골라 바르게 배열하시오. 5점

⚑ 함정

그녀는 타이어를 교체하려고 노력했다.
tried, tires, changing, the, she, change, to

→ _____

U06_3

17 Translate the sentence according to the conditions. 6점

★ 고난도

그들은 바다에서 수영하는 것에 익숙하다.

·Condition 1   8단어로 쓸 것
·Condition 2   3번째 단어는 a로 시작할 것

→ _____

_____

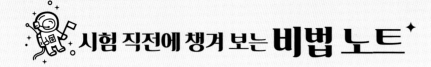

>>> 정답 6쪽

한눈에 쏙! 아래 노트를 보면서 빈칸을 채워 보세요.

1 동명사의 역할

| ¹⁾주_ | ²⁾보_ | ³⁾목__ | ⁴⁾전____ 목__ |

2 동명사 vs. 현재분사

동명사 → ⁂용도, ¹⁾___   현재분사 → ²⁾___, ⁂상태

3 동명사 vs. to부정사

① 동명사를 목적어로 취하는 동사	dislike*, f_____, e_____, m____, g___u_, ə_____, d___
② to부정사를 목적어로 취하는 동사	would like**, wa___, h____, wi___, p____, ə_____, d_____
③ 의미가 달라지는 동사	S___ f_____ and t___ to r_____ before you r_____! (그만 까먹고, 후회하기 전에 기억하려고 노력해라!)

*like는 to부정사/-ing 다 되지만 dislike는 -ing만! **would like는 to부정사만!

헷갈리지 말자! 초록색으로 표시된 부분을 바르게 고쳐 쓰세요.

1 Feel the rain without closed your eyes.

2 Him attending the yoga class was possible.

3 The tourist suggested climbing never the stairs.

4 When we got into the tent, it started rain.

40

CHAPTER 04
시제

UNIT 07 **단순 시제, 현재완료 시제**

UNIT 08 **과거완료 시제, 진행 시제**

UNIT 07 단순 시제, 현재완료 시제

1 단순 시제

어떤 사건이나 동작이 발생한 시간적 위치를 시제라 하며, 과거 시제, 현재 시제, 미래 시제를 단순 시제라 한다.

	내용	예문
현재 시제	현재의 동작, 상태	I study at Stanford University.
	현재의 습관, 반복적 행위	My mom drinks coffee every morning.
	불변의 진리, 사실, 격언	Water freezes at 0℃ and boils at 100℃.
과거 시제	과거의 동작, 상태	It snowed a lot last winter.
	역사적 사실	King Sejong created Hangeul in 1443.
미래 시제	미래에 일어날 동작, 상태	It will be sunny this weekend.
	주어의 의지 표현	I will finish the work today.
	계획, 예정	They are going to play soccer after school.

2 현재 시제가 미래를 나타내는 경우

시간·조건의 부사절	when, before, after절	When he arrives home, I'll call you.
	if절	If the weather is fine, I will go out.
왕래·발착 동사 +미래 부사구	go, come	He comes[is coming] back home tomorrow.
	leave, arrive	She leaves[is leaving] for L.A. next week.

3 현재완료 시제

과거에 일어난 일이 현재까지 영향을 미치는 시제를 현재완료 시제라 한다. 현재완료의 형태는 'have+p.p.'이다.

	의미	자주 함께 쓰이는 표현	예문
완료	막 ~했다	just, already, yet	I have just finished the report.
경험	~한 적이 있다	ever, never, before, once, twice	I've never seen a UFO.
계속	~해 오고 있다	for, since, how long	How long have you stayed here?
결과	~해버렸다 (그래서 지금은 …하다)	go, come, leave, lose, buy	Elvis has left the building.

GRAMMAR POINT

명사절과 형용사절의 미래 시제

- 명사절과 형용사절에서는 미래를 나타낼 때 미래 시제로 쓴다.

I don't know when he will come.

(명사절: 나는 그가 언제 올지 모른다.)

Do you know if he will come?

(명사절: 그가 올지 알고 있니?)

I look forward to the day when we will meet again.

(형용사절: 나는 우리가 다시 만날 날을 손꼽아 기다린다.)

현재완료에서 for와 since

- for+기간

We have waited for 2 hours.

- since+과거 시점

It has not rained since last week.

- since+주어+동사

He has lived there since he was a little kid.

현재완료와 함께 쓸 수 없는 것

- 명백한 과거를 나타내는 부사(구): yesterday, last, ago, then, just now

He has arrived in Busan yesterday. (×)

→ He arrived in Busan yesterday. (○)

- 의문사 when과 함께 쓸 수 없다.

When have you eaten Mexican food? (×)

→ When did you eat Mexican food? (○)

have been/gone to

- have been to(경험): ~에 가본 적 있다

They have been to Cuba. (They're not in Cuba; they're here now.)

- have gone to(결과): ~에 가버렸다

They have gone to Cuba. (They're in Cuba, so they're not here now.)

VOCA Stanford University 스탠포드 대학교 | ℃ (degree(s) Celsius) 섭씨 온도 | create 만들다 | UFO (= unidentified flying object) 미확인 비행 물체

Let's Check It Out

My score is / 17점

A [ ]에서 알맞은 것을 고르시오. 각 1점

1 She often [goes / is going] to the theater.
2 The car [hits / hit] my bike yesterday.
3 It [is / will be] foggy tomorrow morning.
4 If it [is / will be] rainy tomorrow, I will stay home.
5 When I [will arrive / arrive] home, I'll call you.
6 My mom doesn't know when I [will arrive / arrive] at the airport.

B [ ]에서 알맞은 것을 고르시오. 각 1점

1 I [have owned / owned] these jeans for three years.
2 Bill [has been / has gone] to Brazil several times, so he knows a lot about the country.
3 Dad [cleaned / has cleaned] his car since this morning.
4 He [didn't see / hasn't seen] her the day before yesterday.
5 She [has been / has gone] to China. She isn't in Seoul now.

C 어법상 어색한 부분이 있으면 바르게 고쳐 쓰시오. 각 1점

1 I'll buy you a snack if you will help me.

   _____ ➡ _____

2 We will start the performance after the actors arrive.

   _____ ➡ _____

3 I'm not sure if he drops by again tomorrow.

   _____ ➡ _____

4 They have enjoyed watching a movie since two hours.

   _____ ➡ _____

5 He was sick since yesterday.

   _____ ➡ _____

6 I have gone to Singapore before.

   _____ ➡ _____

VOCA **foggy** 안개 낀 | **own** 소유하다, 가지다 | **the day before yesterday** 그제 | **snack** 과자 | **performance** 공연 | **drop by** 들르다

1 빈칸에 알맞은 말이 순서대로 나열된 것은? 2점

> It has been _____ all day, and it _____ yet.

① rained – have stopped   ② rained – has stopped

③ raining – have stopped   ④ raining – hasn't stopped

⑤ rained – hasn't stopped

2 같은 용법의 현재완료가 쓰인 문장을 바르게 묶은 사람은? (답 2개) 3점

> ⓐ It has snowed since yesterday.
> ⓑ Have you ever heard about the disease?
> ⓒ They have already made the food.
> ⓓ Have you called your mom yet?
> ⓔ How many times have you seen a whale?

① 주호: ⓐ, ⓔ   ② 찬미: ⓑ, ⓓ   ③ 미소: ⓒ, ⓓ

④ 소라: ⓑ, ⓔ   ⑤ 라나: ⓒ, ⓔ

3 주어진 조건에 맞게 문장을 영작하시오. 4점

> 태양은 동쪽으로 떠서 서쪽으로 진다.
>
> ·조건1 어휘 – the sun, rise, set, east, west
> ·조건2 11단어로 쓸 것

→ _____

4 Look at the picture and complete the sentence by using the present perfect tense. 4점

miss, just, the train

→ The man _____ .

과거완료 시제, 진행 시제

 1 과거완료 시제

	의미	예문
완료	막 ~했었다	He had just finished the work when I arrived.
경험	~한 적이 있었다	I had never seen a dolphin before I came here.
계속	~해 오고 있었다	How long had you waited there until you met him?
결과	~해버렸었다	I had lost my wallet, so I couldn't pay for the meal.

2 진행 시제

현재 진행형	am/are/is+-ing ~하고 있는 중이다	I am eating lunch now.
과거 진행형	was/were+-ing ~하고 있는 중이었다	Were you studying at that time?
현재완료 진행형	have/has been+-ing ~해 오고 있는 중이다	He has been playing soccer for three hours.
과거완료 진행형	had been+-ing ~해 왔던 중이었다	I had been sleeping for 12 hours when my mom woke me up.

3 동사의 12 시제

	기본 시제	He writes a poem. (그는 시를 쓴다.)
현재	진행	He is writing a poem. (그는 시를 쓰고 있다.)
	완료	He has written a poem. (그는 막 시를 썼다. / 그는 시를 쓴 적이 있다. / 그는 시를 써 왔다.)
	완료 진행	He has been writing a poem. (그는 시를 써 오고 있는 중이다.)
	기본 시제	He wrote a poem. (그는 시를 썼다.)
과거	진행	He was writing a poem. (그는 시를 쓰고 있었다.)
	완료	He had written a poem. (그는 막 시를 썼었다. / 그는 시를 쓴 적이 있었다. / 그는 시를 써 왔었다.)
	완료 진행	He had been writing a poem. (그는 시를 써 오고 있는 중이었다.)
	기본 시제	He will write a poem. (그는 시를 쓸 것이다.)
미래	진행	He will be writing a poem. (그는 시를 쓰고 있을 것이다.)
	완료	He will have written a poem. (그는 시를 썼을 것이다.)
	완료 진행	He will have been writing a poem. (그는 시를 써 오고 있었을 것이다.)

GRAMMAR POINT

과거완료 시제란?

• 과거의 어느 때를 기준으로 그 전에 발생한 사건이 과거의 기준 시점까지 영향을 미치는 시제를 과거완료 시제라 한다. 또한 과거의 두 사건 중 먼저 일어난 일을 시간적으로 구분할 때도 과거완료(대과거) 시제를 쓴다.

과거완료 대신 과거를 쓰는 경우

• before, after와 같이 시간의 전후 관계가 명백한 접속사가 있을 때는 과거완료 대신 과거 시제를 쓸 수 있다.

After I breathed[had breathed] the cool air, I felt fresh.

The students arrived[had arrived] in the classroom before the teacher came.

진행형으로 쓰지 않는 동사

• 소유(have, own, belong to), 감정(like, hate), 인식(know, understand) 등을 나타내는 동사는 진행형으로 쓰지 않는다.

She is having (→ has) blond hair.

Now I am understanding (→ understand) your explanation.

• have가 소유 외의 의미일 경우에는 진행형으로 쓸 수 있다.

I couldn't answer the phone because I was taking a shower.

VOCA **wallet** 지갑 | **pay for** ~의 값을 치르다 | **breathe** 호흡하다 | **wake up** 깨우다 | **belong to** ~에 속하다 | **blond** 금발의 | **explanation** 설명 |
poem 시

Let's Check It Out

>>> 정답 6쪽

A [ ]에서 알맞은 것을 고르시오. 각 1점

1 The bus [has left / had left] when I got to the bus stop.

2 She lost the encyclopedia that I [has lent / had lent] to her.

3 It [has rained / had rained] a lot right before you came here.

4 They [have arrived / had arrived] at the house before we cleaned the mess.

B 우리말과 뜻이 같도록 괄호 안의 단어를 빈칸에 알맞은 형태로 쓰시오. 각 1점

1 너는 어제 저녁 8시에 쇼핑하고 있었니? (shop)

→ _____ _____ _____ at 8 o'clock last night?

2 그는 두 시간 동안 스마트폰으로 게임을 하고 있는 중이다. (play)

→ He _____ _____ _____ games on his smartphone for two hours.

3 나는 10살 때부터 일본어를 배우고 있다. (learn)

→ I _____ _____ _____ Japanese since I was 10 years old.

4 나는 어제 나의 첫 번째 차를 팔았다. 나는 19살 이후로 그 차를 계속 몰아오고 있었다. (drive)

→ I sold my first car yesterday. I _____ _____ _____ it since I was 19 years old.

C 밑줄 친 부분을 괄호 안의 시제로 바꿔 쓰시오. 각 1점

1 He teaches coding. (현재 진행형) → _____

2 They ran on the treadmill. (과거 진행형) → _____

3 She sang the same song for an hour. (현재완료) → _____

4 I found the ring that I lost before. (과거완료) → _____

5 It has snowed since yesterday. (현재완료 진행형) → _____

VOCA encyclopedia 백과사전 | mess 엉망인 상태 | coding 코딩 | treadmill 러닝머신

46

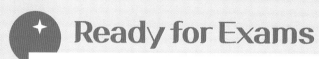

Ready for Exams

>>> 정답 6쪽

My score is

Let's Check It Out _____ / 13점   0~17점 → Level 1 Test
Ready for Exams _____ / 12점 ➡ 18~21점 → Level 2 Test
Total _____ / 25점   22~25점 → Level 3 Test

1 빈칸에 알맞은 동사의 형태는? 2점

> I lost the new drone that my mom _____ for me.

① brings   ② has bought   ③ had bought
④ was bought   ⑤ was buying

2 Which correction is right? 2점

> They have been married for ten years before they moved here.

① have been → had been
② have been → have being
③ for → since
④ moved → will move
⑤ moved → had moved

3 Fill in the blanks with the proper words. 4점

> I have a twin sister. We were born together. We are still together.

→ My twin sister and I _____ _____ together ever
 since we were born.

4 괄호 안의 단어를 활용하여 다음 두 상황을 하나의 문장으로 나타낼 때 빈칸에 알맞은 말을
 쓰시오. 4점

• 2010   • 2020

I started to learn English in 2010.
I moved to Boston in 2020.

→ I _____ _____ English for 10 years before I
 _____ to Boston. (learn, move)

VOCA   drone 드론 | married 결혼한, 기혼의 | twin 쌍둥이; 쌍둥이의

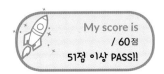

>>> 정답 7쪽

U07_1

01 다음 대화의 빈칸에 들어갈 말로 알맞은 것은? 2점

A: What does Ann usually do at dawn?
B: She usually _____ meditation.

① practice
② practices
③ is practicing
④ will practice
⑤ was practicing

U07_1+2+GP

02 How many sentences are incorrect? 4점

★ 고난도

ⓐ She will go to the exhibition if she will have time.
ⓑ He is going to school soon.
ⓒ Ted has finished the work just now.
ⓓ The teacher said water froze at 0°C.

① none
② one
③ two
④ three
⑤ four

U07_1+3

03 괄호 안의 단어를 활용하여 문장을 완성할 때, 빈칸에 알맞은 말이 순서대로 연결된 것은? 3점

• The rumor has already _____ around the school. (spread)
• They didn't get _____ in the end. (marry)

① spread – marry
② spread – married
③ spreaded – married
④ spreaded – marry
⑤ spreading – marry

U07_3

04 빈칸에 알맞은 말을 고르시오. 2점

A: Where is John?
B: He is not here. He _____ the mall.

① has been to
② had been in
③ have been to
④ has gone to
⑤ had gone to

U07_3+GP

05 Which explanation is correct? 2점

ⓐ When have you been to Japan?
ⓑ She has met him a week ago.
ⓒ Her son has been invited to the party.

① ⓐ: when은 과거 시제에만 쓰인다.
② ⓐ: when은 미래 시제에만 쓰인다.
③ ⓑ: ago는 완료 시제와 함께 쓰일 수 없다.
④ ⓑ: a week ago를 since a week로 바꿔야 한다.
⑤ ⓒ: has been invite로 바꾸어야 올바른 문장이다.

U07_1+U08_2

06 다음 빈칸에 들어갈 알맞은 말은? 2점

I _____ to pop songs since I was very young, so I know lots of songs.

① listen
② listened
③ will listen
④ was listening
⑤ have listened

U08_2

07 주어진 우리말을 영어로 바르게 옮긴 것은? 2점

너는 8년 동안 계속 수학 공부를 해 오고 있니?

① Has you studying math for 8 years?
② You have studying math for 8 years?
③ Have you studying math for 8 years?
④ You has been studying math for 8 years?
⑤ Have you been studying math for 8 years?

U08_1

08 Which is correct for the blank when combining the two sentences into one? 3점

I lost my watch in the park yesterday. I found the watch today.
→ I found the watch which I _____ in the park.

① was lost
② have lost
③ had been losing
④ have been losing
⑤ had lost

09 U07_1

Rewrite the sentence correctly. 5점

함정

> Tony is resembling his mother.

→ _____

10 U07_3

조건에 맞게 다음 두 문장의 의미를 포함할 수 있는 한 문장을 쓰시오. 6점

> My niece went to Paris last year. She still lives there now.
>
> · 조건 1 어휘 – live, since, in
> · 조건 2 빈칸에 7단어로 쓸 것

→ My niece _____

_____ .

11 U08_GP

어법상 어색한 부분을 찾아 바르게 고치시오. 6점

★ 고난도

> I have been knowing him since he was a baby.

_____ → _____

12 U07_2+GP

다음 중 어법상 어색한 문장을 찾아 바르게 고치시오. 4점

> ⓐ I wonder if she stays home tomorrow.
> ⓑ If you leave me now, I won't see you again.

(   ) _____ → _____

13 U08_3

다음 우리말과 일치하도록 주어진 단어를 활용하여 문장을 완성하시오. 4점

> 나는 이번 주가 끝날 때면 모든 기말시험을 치렀을 것이다. (take)

→ I _____ all of my final exams by the end of this week.

14 U08_2

Fill in the blanks by using the given word. 5점

> A: Hello. What are you doing here?
> B: I'm waiting to see the manager. I _____ _____ _____ for half an hour. (wait)

15 U08_1

다음은 소설 '어린 왕자'의 일부이다. 조건에 맞게 빈칸을 채우시오. 각 5점

함정

> "If you please, draw me a sheep..." I told the little prince that I didn't know how to draw. He answered me, "That doesn't matter. Draw me a sheep..." But I ____(A)____ a sheep. (그러나 나는 양을 그려 본 적이 없었다.) So I drew for him one of the two pictures I ____(B)____ so often. (그래서 나는 내가 그토록 자주 그려 왔던 두 가지 그림 중에서 하나를 그에게 그려 주었다.) It was an elephant inside a boa constrictor.
>
> *boa constrictor: 보아뱀
>
> · 조건 두 문장 모두 draw동사를 활용할 것

(A) _____

(B) _____

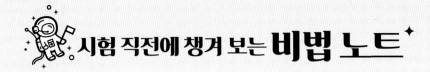

>>> 정답 7쪽

한눈에 쏙! 아래 노트를 보면서 빈칸을 채워 보세요.

1 기본 시제와 진행* 시제

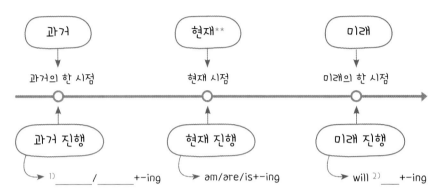

> 과거 → 과거의 한 시점
> 현재** → 현재 시점
> 미래 → 미래의 한 시점
>
> 과거 진행 → 1) _____ / _____ +-ing
> 현재 진행 → am/are/is+-ing
> 미래 진행 → will 2) ____ +-ing

*진행형 쓸 수 없는 동사: have(가지고 있다), like, know **때·조건 부사절에서 현재가 3) _____의 뜻

2 완료 시제와 완료 진행 시제

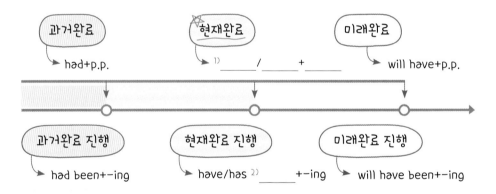

> 과거완료 → had+p.p.
> 현재완료 → 1) _____ / _____ + _____
> 미래완료 → will have+p.p.
>
> 과거완료 진행 → had been+-ing
> 현재완료 진행 → have/has 2) _____ +-ing
> 미래완료 진행 → will have been+-ing

헷갈리지 말자! 초록색으로 표시된 부분을 바르게 고쳐 쓰세요.

1 I have been to Europe last year.

2 My sister is having blue eyes.

3 I have studied a lot before I started using social media.

CHAPTER 05
조동사

UNIT 09 **조동사(1)**

UNIT 10 **조동사(2)**

UNIT 09 조동사(1)

CONCEPT 1 can, may, will, must, should

조동사	의미	긍정	부정
can	능력, 가능	~할 수 있다 (= be able to)	cannot[can't]: ~할 수 없다 (= be not able to)
	허락	~해도 된다 (= may)	~하면 안 된다 (= may not)
may	약한 추측	~일지도 모른다	may not: ~이 아닐지도 모른다
	허락	~해도 된다 (= can)	~하면 안 된다 (= cannot)
will	미래	~할 것이다 (= be going to)	will not[won't]: ~하지 않을 것이다 (= be not going to)
must	의무/불필요	~해야 한다 (= have/has to)	① don't/doesn't have to: ~할 필요 없다 (= don't/doesn't need to, need not) ② must not[mustn't]: ~해서는 안 된다
	강한 추측(확신)	~임에 틀림없다	cannot[can't]: ~일 리가 없다
should	도덕적 의무, 충고, 조언	~해야 한다 (= ought to)	should not[shouldn't]: ~해서는 안 된다 (= ought not to)

CONCEPT 2 can, may가 사용된 중요 표현

cannot help+-ing ~하지 않을 수 없다	She was so sad that she could not help crying. (그녀는 너무 슬퍼서 울지 않을 수 없었다.)
cannot... without+-ing …할 때마다 꼭 ~하게 되다	They cannot meet without fighting. (그들은 만나면 꼭 싸운다.)
cannot ~ too... 아무리 …해도 지나치지 않다, 반드시 …해야 한다	People cannot be too careful when driving a car. (차를 운전할 때는 반드시 주의해야 한다.)
may[might] well+동사원형 ~하는 것이 당연하다	She may well be proud of her daughter. (그녀는 딸을 자랑스러워하는 것이 당연하다.)
may[might] as well+동사원형 ~하는 편이 낫다	You may as well keep the money. (너는 그 돈을 간직하는 편이 낫다.)
may[might] as well A as B B 하기보다는 A 하는 편이 낫다	You may as well go as stay. (너는 머무르느니 떠나는 게 낫다.)

CONCEPT 3 that절에서 should의 생략

A suggest(제안), insist(주장), demand(요구), order(명령), advise(충고)

He suggested that we (should) leave earlier.

B 이성적 판단: It is important, necessary, essential, natural, strange, a pity

It is essential that students (should) have a book in class.

GRAMMAR POINT

조동사의 과거형
- can → could
- may → might
- will → would
- must(의무) → had to

would의 두 가지 쓰임
- 시제 일치(~할 것이다)

  He said that he would come to see me.
- 과거의 불규칙적인 습관(~하곤 했다)

  He would go fishing with his dad when he was a child.

cannot but + 동사원형
- cannot help+-ing는 「cannot (help) but+동사원형」(~하지 않을 수 없다)로 바꿔 쓸 수 있다.

  She was so sad that she could not help crying.
  → She was so sad that she could not but cry.

whenever
- cannot... without+-ing는 whenever(~할 때마다)를 사용해서 바꿔 쓸 수 있다.

  They cannot meet without fighting.
  → Whenever they meet, they fight.

VOCA proud 자랑스러운 | necessary 필요한 | essential 필수적인 | natural 자연스러운 | strange 이상한

Let's Check It Out

》》》 정답 7쪽

My score is

/ 14점

A 두 문장의 뜻이 같도록 빈칸에 알맞은 말을 쓰시오. 각 1점

1 You don't have to bring him this document.

→ You _____ _____ bring him this document.

2 He will not go shopping this weekend.

→ He _____ _____ _____ go shopping this weekend.

3 You shouldn't talk loudly in public places.

→ You _____ _____ _____ talk loudly in public places.

4 She is tired and cannot help resting.

→ She is tired and _____ but _____.

B 우리말과 같은 뜻이 되도록 괄호 안의 말을 활용하여 빈칸에 알맞게 쓰시오. 각 1점

1 소라가 아플 리가 없다. (sick, be, can't)

→ Sora _____.

2 당신은 여기서 떠들면 안 된다. (make any noise, may)

→ You _____ here.

3 나는 클래식 음악을 들으면 꼭 잔다. (cannot, listen to, fall asleep)

→ I _____ classical music _____.

4 그녀가 그렇게 말하는 것은 당연하다. (may, say)

→ She _____ that.

5 길을 건널 때 아무리 주의해도 지나치지 않다. (cannot, careful)

→ You _____ when crossing a street.

C [ ]에서 알맞은 것을 고르시오. 각 1점

1 Do you think I [should / ought] to obey the rule?

2 You [should / ought] not despise the poor.

3 He suggested that I [would / should] finish the project.

4 When you go to a high school entrance ceremony, you [would / should] wear your school uniform.

5 It's a pity that Alice [shall / should] marry such a man.

VOCA document 서류 | rest 쉬다 | obey 따르다, 복종하다 | despise 경멸하다 | the poor 가난한 사람들 | entrance ceremony 입학식

Ready for Exams

My score is

Let's Check It Out _____ / 14점

Ready for Exams _____ / 11점

Total _____ / 25점

0~17점 → Level 1 Test

18~21점 → Level 2 Test

22~25점 → Level 3 Test

1 밑줄 친 부분의 쓰임이 같은 것끼리 모두 묶인 것은? 2점

ⓐ She <u>may</u> still be crying.
ⓑ The story <u>may</u> not be true.
ⓒ My mom <u>may</u> be late tonight.
ⓓ Santa <u>may</u> give a gift to you.
ⓔ You <u>may</u> go out if you want.

① ⓐ, ⓑ, ⓔ
② ⓑ, ⓒ, ⓓ
③ ⓑ, ⓓ, ⓔ
④ ⓒ, ⓓ, ⓔ
⑤ ⓐ, ⓑ, ⓒ, ⓓ

2 Choose ALL the correct words for the blank. 2점

It is necessary that he _____ regularly.

① exercise
② exercises
③ exercised
④ could exercise
⑤ should exercise

3 다음 두 문장의 의미가 같도록 빈칸에 알맞은 말을 쓰시오. 3점

Children should not eat too much chocolate.

→ Children _____ _____ _____ eat too much chocolate.

4 Translate the sentence according to the conditions. 4점

우리는 그가 자신의 실수를 인정해야 한다고 주장했다.

· 조건 1 어휘 – insist, admit, mistake
· 조건 2 조동사는 쓰지 말 것
· 조건 3 7단어로 쓸 것

→ _____

VOCA necessary 필요한 | regularly 규칙적으로 | admit 인정하다

54

10 조동사(2)

CONCEPT 1 would like to, had better, used to

조동사	긍정	부정
would like to	~하고 싶다 (= want to) I would like to apologize.	would not[wouldn't] like to: ~하고 싶지 않다 I wouldn't like to take part in the contest.
had better	~하는 것이 좋겠다 (충고, 제안) You had better yield to pedestrians.	had better not: ~하지 않는 것이 좋겠다 You had better not give up.
would rather	~하는 것이 낫겠다 (선택) I would rather stay home. would rather A than B (= prefer A to B): B 하느니 차라리 A 하는 것이 낫다	would rather not: ~하지 않는 것이 낫겠다 I would rather not stay home.
used to	① 과거의 습관: ~하곤 했다 On weekends, we used to go camping. ② 과거의 상태: 예전에 ~이었다 There used to be a tree in the yard, but now there isn't.	didn't use to (드물게 used not to) We didn't use to go camping. There did not use to be a tree, but now there is.
would	과거의 습관: ~하곤 했다 I would cry when my mom scolded me.	

CONCEPT 2 조동사 + have + p.p.

	의미	부정
should have + p.p.	~했어야 했다 (후회·유감)	should not have + p.p.
may[might] have + p.p.	~했을지도 모른다 (약한 추측)	may[might] not have + p.p.
must have + p.p.	~했음에 틀림없다 (강한 추측)	cannot have + p.p. (~했을 리가 없다)

I couldn't help him. I should have come earlier.
(나는 그를 도와주지 못했다. 내가 더 일찍 왔어야만 했다.)

Carl looks tired. He may have been awake all night.
(Carl은 피곤해 보인다. 그는 밤새 깨어 있었을지도 모른다.)

Tom got a perfect score. He must have studied hard.
(Tom이 만점을 받았다. 그는 열심히 공부했음에 틀림없다.)

He cannot have sent me a message. I didn't get anything.
(그가 나에게 메시지를 보냈을 리가 없다. 나는 아무것도 받지 못했다.)

GRAMMAR POINT

had better의 주어
• had better는 주로 2인칭 주어 (you)와 함께 사용되며, 1인칭 주어(I, we)와도 자주 사용된다.
You had better follow her advice.
I'd better go now.

would rather의 주어
• would rather는 주로 1인칭 주어와 함께 사용된다.
I would rather sleep than read a boring book.

used to + 동사원형
• 과거의 습관이나 상태를 나타내며, 현재는 그렇지 않다는 의미를 내포한다.
My father used to smoke.
(지금은 아버지가 담배를 피우지 않는다는 의미)

used to의 의문문 형태
• used to의 의문문 형태는 「Did + 주어 + use to + 동사원형 ~?」 또는 「Did there use to be ~?」이다.
Did you use to live in the country?
Did there use to be a tree here?

used to의 세 가지 쓰임
• used to + 동사원형: ~하곤 했다
I used to get up late.
• be used to + -ing: ~하는 것에 익숙하다
I am used to sleeping on the bus.
• be used to + 동사원형: ~하기 위해 사용되다
The cart is used to carry bananas.

VOCA apologize 사과하다 | yield 양보하다 | pedestrian 보행자 | yard 뜰, 정원 | country 시골 | cart 카트 | perfect score 만점 | send(-sent-sent) 보내다

>>> 정답 8쪽

A 우리 말과 같은 뜻이 되도록 괄호 안의 말을 빈칸에 배열하시오. 각 1점

  1 너는 잠자리에 들기 전에 샤워하는 것이 낫겠다. (better, had, take)

  → You _____ a shower before going to bed.

  2 우리 마을에는 작은 교회가 있었어. (be, to, used)

  → There _____ a small church in my village.

  3 나는 그를 만나고 싶다. (would, to, meet, like)

  → I _____ him.

B 어법상 어색한 부분을 바르게 고쳐 쓰시오. 각 1점

  1 You had better to go immediately.

  _____ → _____

  2 I would rather live in a small town as in a big city.

  _____ → _____

  3 You had not better say anything.

  _____ → _____

  4 I am used to swim in cold water.

  _____ → _____

  5 I would rather starve to death than stealing.

  _____ → _____

C 빈칸에 알맞은 말을 [보기]에서 골라 쓰시오. 각 1점

보기	should	might	must	cannot

  1 너는 열심히 공부했어야 했다.

  → You _____ have studied hard.

  2 그들은 그때 놀고 있었음에 틀림없다.

  → They _____ have played then.

  3 그가 그것에 대한 돈을 지불했을 리가 없다.

  → He _____ have paid for it.

  4 그녀는 자고 있었을지도 모른다.

  → She _____ have been sleeping.

VOCA take a shower 샤워하다 | village 마을 | immediately 즉시

1   Which is suitable for the blank? 2점

I _____ play in the stream when I was young.

① will   ② can   ③ have to

④ used to   ⑤ had better

2   빈칸에 알맞은 말은? 2점

The kids were very polite. They _____ have been well educated.

① must   ② should   ③ cannot

④ will   ⑤ would

3   Find the sentence that has an error and correct it. 3점

ⓐ You had not better go camping tomorrow.
ⓑ I would not like to eat at that restaurant.

(   ) _____ ➡ _____

4   그림을 보고 주어진 어휘와 조건에 맞게 대화의 밑줄 친 (A)와 (B)를 영작하시오. 각 3점

Mom: Sweetie, did you take your umbrella?
Son: No, I didn't.
Mom: (A) 우산을 가져갔어야지. I told you it was going to rain, didn't I?
Son: I know. (B) 엄마 말씀을 들었어야 했어요.

· 어휘 take one's umbrella, listen to
· 조건 (A)와 (B) 각각 6단어로 쓸 것

(A) _____

(B) _____

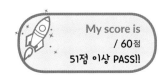

>>> 정답 8쪽

U09_1

01 다음 대화의 빈칸에 알맞은 것을 <u>모두</u> 고르시오. 2점

> A: Do I have to ask you for permission?
> B: _____. You can do what you want.

① Yes, you must
② Yes, you have to
③ No, you won't
④ No, you don't have to
⑤ No, you need not

U10_1

02 다음 우리말을 영어로 바르게 옮긴 것은? 2점

> 너는 좀 더 정확히 쓰는 게 좋겠다.

① You would like to write more accurately.
② You had better write more accurately.
③ You must write more accurately.
④ You had like to write more accurately.
⑤ You want to write more accurately.

U10_1

03 다음 문장을 올바르게 고친 학생은? 2점

> He didn't use take a nap.

① 민희: didn't use는 used not으로 바꾸어야 해.
② 철수: didn't use는 didn't used로 바꾸어야 해.
③ 지우: take는 to take로 바꾸어야 해.
④ 영희: take는 taking로 바꾸어야 해.
⑤ 수지: didn't use는 don't use to로 바꾸어야 해.

U09_3

04 Which correction is right? 3점

 함정

> It was essential that he carried water in the hot desert.

① carried → carry
② carried → carrying
③ carried → carries
④ was → is
⑤ that → if

U09_2+3

05 Which sentences are grammatically <u>incorrect</u>? 4점

★ 고난도

> ⓐ Dana demanded we find another way.
> ⓑ The doctor suggested that she eats more vegetables and less meat.
> ⓒ You may well saving energy by turning the lights off.
> ⓓ I cannot help regretting what happened.

① ⓐ, ⓑ, ⓒ   ② ⓐ, ⓒ
③ ⓐ, ⓓ   ④ ⓑ, ⓒ
⑤ ⓑ, ⓓ

U10_2

06 다음 문장과 같은 의미의 문장은? (답 2개) 2점

> It is possible that the criminal hid in a temple.

① The criminal might have hidden in a temple.
② The criminal might hide in a temple.
③ The criminal must have hidden in a temple.
④ The criminal may have hidden in a temple.
⑤ The criminal may hide in a temple.

U10_1

07 우리말을 영어로 바르게 옮긴 것은? 2점

> 나는 밖에 나가느니 차라리 공부를 하겠다.

① I'd rather study than go out.
② I'd rather study to go out.
③ I'd rather go out than study.
④ I'd rather go out to study.
⑤ I'd rather studying than going out.

U09_2+GP

08 다음 중 어법상 <u>어색한</u> 것을 찾아 바르게 고친 것은? 3점

◉ 한눈에 쏙

> ⓐ I couldn't help weep at the sad movie.
> ⓑ I cannot but weep at the sad movie.

① ⓐ couldn't → can't
② ⓐ weep → weeping
③ ⓐ weep → to weep
④ ⓑ but → help
⑤ ⓑ weep → weeping

Challenge! 주관식 서술형

U09_1

09 다음 글의 흐름에 맞게 빈칸 (A)에 <u>필요한 어휘만</u> 골라 배열하시오. 4점

> _____(A)_____ in this lane. It is for pedestrians.
> (don't, your bike, have, not, must, you, ride)

(A) _____

U09_1

10 ★고난도 다음 우리말을 조건에 맞게 영작하시오. 5점

> 우리는 그때 그것에 대해 논쟁할 필요가 없었다.
> ・조건 1 어휘 – argue about, then
> ・조건 2 8단어로 쓸 것

→ _____

U09_1

11 Rearrange the words in the correct order. 4점

> be, not, ought, to, allowed, such, things

→ _____

U09_3

12 다음 문장에서 어법상 <u>어색한 부분</u>을 바르게 고쳐 문장을 다시 쓰시오. 4점

> The doctor suggested that I drank a lot of water.

→ _____

U09_2

13 함정 Rearrange the words correctly to translate the sentence. 5점

> 나는 그 식은 피자를 먹느니 저녁을 굶는 게 낫겠다.
> I, well, as, cold, eat, may, the, pizza, as, skip, dinner

→ _____

U09_2+U10_1

14 다음과 같은 의미의 문장을 조건에 맞게 쓰시오. 4점

> You had better stop smoking.
> ・조건 may를 넣을 것

→ _____

U09_3

15 ★고난도 다음 그림을 보고 조건에 맞게 영작하시오. 5점

> 미녀(Beauty)가 야수와 결혼해야 하는 것은 안타까운 일이다.
> ・조건 1 어휘 – a pity, marry the beast
> ・조건 2 조동사를 쓸 것
> ・조건 3 9단어로 쓸 것

→ _____

U10_2

16 함정 Complete the sentence to have the same meaning as the one in the box. 5점

> I regret that I didn't focus on the test.

→ I _____ _____
   _____ on the test.

U10_1

17 조건에 맞게 다음을 영작하시오. 4점

> 그 드라마는 너무 슬퍼서 나는 그것을 다시 보고 싶지 않아.
> ・조건 1 어휘 – soap opera, would, watch
> ・조건 2 so ~ that... 구문을 쓸 것

→ _____

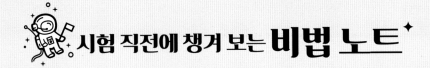
한눈에 쏙! 아래 노트를 보면서 빈칸을 채워 보세요.

1 조동사 형태

조동사 + 1)_____

2 의무, 금지, 불필요

① 의무(~해야 한다)	must, have/has to, should, ought to
② 금지 (1)_____)	2)____ not, may not, cannot, should not, ought not to
③ 불필요 (3)_____)	don't/doesn't 4)____ to = don't/doesn't need to = 5)_____ not

3 중요 조동사 표현

- cannot help+-ing = cannot 1)_____+동사원형(뜻: 2)_____)
- may well+동사원형(뜻: ~하는 것이 당연하다)
- 3)_____ _____ _____+동사원형(뜻: 4)_____)
- used to+동사원형(뜻: ~하곤 했다)
- 5)_____ used to+-ing(뜻: ~하는 데 익숙하다)
- should have+p.p.: 후회(뜻: 6)_____)
- must have+p.p.: 추측(뜻: 7)_____)
- suggest/insist (that)+주어+(8)_____)+9)_____

헷갈리지 말자! 초록색으로 표시된 부분을 바르게 고쳐 쓰세요.

1 Must I get up early tomorrow? – No, you <u>must not</u> get up early. You can sleep in.

2 The pie smelled so delicious. I <u>couldn't help have</u> it.

3 He <u>had not better</u> clean the toaster until he unplugs it.

CHAPTER 06
수동태

UNIT 11 **조동사, 진행형, 완료형의 수동태**

UNIT 12 **여러 가지 수동태**

UNIT 11 조동사, 진행형, 완료형의 수동태

CONCEPT 1 수동태의 의미와 기본 형태

기본형	be + p.p. + by + 행위자
전환법	주어 동사 목적어 주어 / be + p.p. / by + 목적격
의미	주어가 ~이/-히/-지/-되다

Tom painted the fence. → The fence was painted by Tom.

CONCEPT 2 조동사의 수동태

기본형	조동사 + be + p.p.
can, may, must, will, shall, could, might, would, should	can, may, must, will, shall, could, might, would, should ⌐ + be + p.p.

Her sculpture will attract many visitors.

→ Many visitors will be attracted by her sculpture.

CONCEPT 3 진행형의 수동태

기본형	be being + p.p.
현재 진행 수동태	am/is/are being + p.p.
과거 진행 수동태	was/were being + p.p.

The part-time worker is cleaning the door.

→ The door is being cleaned by the part-time worker.

They were destroying the old dam.

→ The old dam was being destroyed (by them).

CONCEPT 4 완료형의 수동태

기본형	have been + p.p.
현재완료 수동태	have/has been + p.p.
과거완료 수동태	had been + p.p.

The kid has developed a game for everyone.

→ A game for everyone has been developed by the kid.

Your sister had worn those blue shoes.

→ Those blue shoes had been worn by your sister.

GRAMMAR POINT

수동태의 be동사

- 시제는 능동태의 동사에, 인칭과 수는 수동태의 주어에 일치시킨다.

  They built the houses.
  → The houses were built by them.

  시제: 능동태의 built → 과거

  인칭과 수: 수동태의 주어인 The houses → 3인칭 복수

'by + 행위자'의 생략

- 'by + 행위자'가 일반인이거나 불분명하거나 불필요한 경우는 생략 가능하다.

  Spanish is spoken in Mexico (by people). 일반인

  My car was stolen (by someone) last night. 불분명

  I was born and raised in Incheon (by my parents). 불필요

의문문 수동태 전환법

- 의문문의 수동태는 평서문으로 바꾼 후 전환하면 편리하다.

  What did the man do?
  → The man did what?
  → What was done by the man?

be going to be+p.p.

- will be + p.p.는 be going to be + p.p.로도 쓸 수 있다.

  The package will be delivered tomorrow.
  → The package is going to be delivered tomorrow.

have to와 ought to의 수동태

- have to와 ought to의 수동태는 have to be + p.p.와 ought to be + p.p.이다.

  The work has to be done by today.

  The bill ought to be paid now.

VOCA   sculpture 조각품 | attract 끌다 | package 소포 | deliver 배달하다 | destroy 파괴하다 | dam 댐 | develop 개발하다

Let's Check It Out

>>> 정답 9쪽

A [ ]에서 알맞은 것을 고르시오. 각 1점

1 The sitcom [is loved / loves] by almost everyone.
2 Many people [speak / are spoken] English.
3 The report [was written / written] by Mr. Lim.
4 The questions [don't answer / aren't answered] correctly.
5 The dogs [were loving / were loved] by the man.

B 주어진 단어를 활용하여 빈칸에 알맞은 말을 쓰시오. 각 1점

1 The deadline _____ _____ _____ _____ by
   everyone. (should, not, forget)
2 The car is _____ _____ by my kids. (be, wash)
3 The song _____ _____ _____ for the film.
   (have, compose)
4 These flowers _____ _____ without water for seven days.
   (can, live)
5 Before you came, the students _____ _____ _____ in
   different classes. (have, place)

C 주어진 단어를 활용하여 우리말과 일치하도록 빈칸을 채우시오. 각 1점

1 그 축구 경기가 지금 진행되는 중이다. (play)
   → The soccer game _____ _____ _____ now.
2 내 이메일 계정은 다음 봄까지 사용되지 않을 거야. (use)
   → My email account _____ _____ _____ till next
   spring.
3 근로자들이 다리를 건설하는 중이다. (construct)
   → The workers _____ _____ the bridge.
4 부정행위는 내 수업에서 절대 용인되어 온 적이 없다. (accept)
   → Cheating _____ _____ _____ _____ in my
   class.
5 나는 지갑이 분실되었기 때문에 돈이 없었다. (lose)
   → I did not have any money because my wallet _____ _____
   _____.

VOCA sitcom 시트콤 | deadline 마감시간 | compose 작곡하다 | place 배치하다 | account 계정 | construct 건설하다 | cheating 부정행위

Ready for Exams

My score is

Let's Check It Out _____ / 15점   0~20점 → Level 1 Test
Ready for Exams _____ / 15점   21~25점 → Level 2 Test
Total _____ / 30점   26~30점 → Level 3 Test

1 Which is proper for the blank? 2점

> A letter _____ to her by her aunt last week.

① sends   ② sent   ③ sended

④ was sent   ⑤ were sent

2 다음을 영작할 때 5번째 올 단어로 적절한 것은? 4점

> 저 개들은 Justin에 의해 반려동물로 입양될 수도 있다.

① pets   ② dogs   ③ be

④ adopted   ⑤ by

3 다음 문장을 조건에 맞게 수동태로 전환하시오. 3점

> They are releasing the prisoners now.
>
> ·조건 1   진행형의 수동태를 정확히 사용할 것
> ·조건 2   불필요한 2단어는 생략할 것

➡ _____

4 Look at the pictures and fill in the blanks by using the given words. 각 3점

(1) His cell phone _____ just _____
_____. (drop)

(2) It _____ _____ now. (break)

12 여러 가지 수동태

1 5형식 문장의 수동태

목적격 보어	주요 5형식 동사	수동태 전환법
명사, 형용사	make, keep, find, consider, leave, elect, call, name	주어 / 동사 / 목적어 / 명사[형용사] 주어 / be+p.p. / 명사[형용사] / (by+목적격)
to부정사	tell, ask, expect, allow, advise, cause, want, order	주어 / 동사 / 목적어 / to부정사 주어 / be+p.p. / to부정사 / (by+목적격)
동사원형	사역동사: make, have, let	주어 / 사역동사 / 목적어 / 동사원형 주어 / be+p.p. / to+동사원형 / (by+목적격)
동사원형, -ing	지각동사: see, watch, hear, listen to, feel	주어 / 지각동사 / 목적어 / 동사원형[-ing] 주어 / be+p.p. / to+동사원형[-ing] / (by+목적격)

The parents left the baby alone. → The baby was left alone by the parents.

The teacher told them to be quiet. → They were told to be quiet by the teacher.

I saw her enter the store. → She was seen to enter the store by me.

Mom made me wear the shirt. → I was made to wear the shirt by Mom.

2 동사구의 수동태

> 주어 / 동사구 / 목적어
>
> 주어 / be+p.p.+나머지 동사구 / (by+목적격)

They made fun of the boy. → The boy was made fun of by them.

3 that절이 목적어인 경우

자주 쓰이는 동사	전환법
say, think, believe, consider, suppose	주어+동사+that S+V → That S+V be+p.p. (by+목적격) → It is+p.p. (by+목적격)+that S+V → 주어+be+p.p. (by+목적격)+to V

They say that Jeju-do is famous for its beaches.

→ That Jeju-do is famous for its beaches is said (by them). (that 절을 주어로)

→ It is said that Jeju-do is famous for its beaches. (가주어 – 진주어 구문으로)

→ Jeju-do is said to be famous for its beaches. (that 절의 주어를 문장의 주어로)

GRAMMAR POINT

5형식의 수동태에서 유의할 점

- 목적격 보어(명사)는 주어로 전환할 수 없다.

  We call the man Bobo.
  - → Bobo is called the man by us. (×)
  - → The man is called Bobo by us. (○)

- 지각동사의 목적격 보어가 -ing면 그대로 쓴다.

  They heard the girl crying.
  - → The girl was heard crying.

- let과 have의 수동태는 유사 표현인 be allowed to ~와 be asked to ~로 만들어야 한다.

  Mom let me go out.
  - → I was let to go out by Mom. (×)
  - → I was allowed to go out by Mom. (○)

  She had him sing.
  - → He was had to sing by her. (×)
  - → He was asked to sing by her. (○)

자주 쓰이는 동사구

- laugh at: ~을 비웃다
- make fun of: ~을 조롱하다
- take care of[look after, care for]: ~을 돌보다
- pick up: ~을 차로 태우다
- look down on: ~을 경시하다
- look up to: ~을 존경하다
- bring up: ~을 기르다
- pay attention to: ~에 주의를 기울이다
- make use of: ~을 이용하다
- deal with: ~을 다루다

by 이외의 전치사를 쓰는 수동태

- by 이외의 전치사를 쓰는 수동태의 목록은 〈내공 중학영문법 2 개념이해책〉 p. 86 참조.

VOCA enter 들어가다 | allow 허락하다 | consider 여기다 | suppose 가정하다

Let's Check It Out

My score is
/ 16점

A 문장을 수동태로 전환할 때 빈칸에 알맞은 말을 쓰시오. 각 1점

1 The hairdresser cut my hair too short.

→ _____ by the hairdresser.

2 Your food blog makes me hungry.

→ I _____ your food blog.

3 They elected him chairman.

→ _____ (by them).

4 The neighbors called him "the crazy guy."

→ _____ by the neighbors.

5 Mr. Seo advised me to work out regularly.

→ I _____ regularly by Mr. Seo.

B 밑줄 친 부분이 어법상 어색하면 바르게 고치시오. 각 1점

1 I was made <u>wash</u> the dishes by my dad. → _____

2 We were asked <u>to walk</u> upstairs. → _____

3 He wasn't allowed <u>participate</u> in the party. → _____

4 Amy was heard <u>singing</u> in the next room. → _____

C [ ]에서 알맞은 것을 고르시오. 각 1점

1 The soldiers were taken care [of / of by] the nurse.

2 I was picked [by / up by] him at the station.

3 It [is believed / believes] that the singer is staying there.

4 [It / She] was said to be the most frightening person in my town.

5 Sarah's eyes were filled [of / with] tears.

D 괄호 안의 단어를 활용하여 우리말과 뜻이 같도록 빈칸에 알맞은 말을 쓰시오. 각 1점

1 나의 강아지는 적절히 보살펴지지 않았어요. (take, care)

→ My dog _____ _____ _____ _____ properly.

2 행복한 사람들이 행복한 마을을 만든다고 말해진다. (say, make)

→ Happy people _____ _____ _____ _____ a happy village.

VOCA hairdresser 미용사 | elect 선출하다 | chairman 회장 | neighbor 이웃 | advise 충고하다 | work out 운동하다 | regularly 규칙적으로 | upstairs 위층으로 | participate 참가하다 | frightening 무서운 | properly 적절히, 제대로 | village 마을

66

Ready for Exams

>>> 정답 9쪽

1 다음 문장을 수동태로 가장 잘 바꾼 것은? 2점

> The workers painted her house yellow.

① Her house yellow is painted by the workers.
② Her house were painted yellow by the workers.
③ Her house was painted yellow by the workers.
④ Her house yellow was painted by the workers.
⑤ Her house is painted yellow by the workers.

2 Who understands the sentence correctly? 2점

> The boys were made clean the tables by him.

① 규진: 소년들이 자발적으로 탁자를 닦은 거야.
② 상빈: 사역동사가 쓰였으니까 동사원형 clean이 맞아.
③ 하나: clean을 to clean으로 바꿔야 해.
④ 한솔: 능동태 문장으로 전환하면 목적어는 the tables야.
⑤ 다진: 능동태 문장은 He made the tables clean the boys.야.

3 주어진 문장을 수동태로 전환할 때 빈칸에 알맞은 말을 쓰시오. 각 2점

> They thought that the movie was awesome.

(1) That the movie was awesome _____ _____ .

(2) It was thought _____ the movie was awesome.

(3) _____ _____ was thought _____
_____ awesome.

4 Read the situation and complete the sentence. 4점

> Joan and Ken were studying at the library. Joan went out to buy some snacks, and Ken kept studying. Suddenly, Joan's phone started ringing. Ken was embarrassed. He turned the phone off immediately.

→ Joan's phone _____ by Ken.

VOCA awesome 훌륭한, 멋진 | embarrassed 당황한 | immediately 즉시

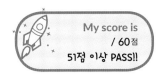
>>> 정답 9쪽

01 'ought to'를 사용해서 다음을 영작할 때 5번째 올 단어로 적절한 것은? 3점

함정

> 이 문제는 너에 의해서 해결되어야 한다.

① solved   ② ought
③ by   ④ to
⑤ be

U11_2

02 다음 밑줄 친 부분을 바르게 고친 것은? 2점

> The children will helped by the gentleman.

① will help   ② will is helping
③ will be helping   ④ will be helped
⑤ is going to help

U11_4

03 Who understands the sentence correctly? 3점

한눈에 쏙

> The tennis match has called off since July.

① 유영: call off의 동사구가 들어간 올바른 수동태야.
② 은수: have+p.p.의 현재완료 수동태 문장이야.
③ 진애: off 다음의 since를 by로 바꿔야 해.
④ 세정: has called off를 is called off로 써야 해.
⑤ 동민: has와 called 사이에 been을 넣어야 해.

U12_1

04 주어진 문장을 수동태로 올바르게 전환한 것은? 2점

> They didn't allow her to perform in the hall.

① She wasn't allowed to perform in the hall.
② She was allowed to perform in the hall.
③ She isn't allowed to perform in the hall.
④ She is allowed to perform in the hall.
⑤ She didn't allow them to perform in the hall.

U12_3

05 다음 문장에서 어색한 것을 찾아 바르게 고친 것은? 2점

> It thinks that the construction is going to be finished next month.

① It → That
② thinks → is thought
③ that → which
④ is going to → is going
⑤ be finished → finish

U11_3

06 다음 밑줄 친 부분을 능동태로 올바르게 전환한 것은? 2점

> I was quite sure I was being followed.

① someone followed me
② I was following someone
③ someone has followed me
④ somebody was followed me
⑤ someone was following me

U11_2+U12_1

07 How many are grammatically incorrect? 4점

고난도

> ⓐ Is the party being prepared by her?
> ⓑ They were made move the rocks.
> ⓒ I know that paper is made from wood.
> ⓓ The work must done immediately.
> ⓔ Busan is said to be crowded with tourists.

① one   ② two
③ three   ④ four
⑤ five

U12_1+GP

08 다음 문장 전환에서 빈칸에 알맞은 말은? (답 2개) 2점

> Caroline watched Jim climb up the tree.
> → Jim was watched _____ up the tree by Caroline.

① climb   ② climbing
③ to climb   ④ climbed
⑤ be climbing

09 U12_2+3
★ 고난도
다음 중 어법상 올바른 문장들의 첫 글자를 따서 아래의 단어를 완성하시오. 6점

ⓐ The boy was laughed by his classmates.
ⓑ Your pet can be healed by this treatment.
ⓒ A cure for the disease has been discovered.
ⓓ The poor should not be looked down upon.
ⓔ It is saying that the work can be done soon.

→ □ □ C H □

10 U11_2
다음 문장을 수동태로 전환하시오. 5점

She had to walk the dogs.

→ _____

11 U11_3+U12_2
✔ 함정
Look at the picture and answer the question starting with the given words. 5점

Q: Are the students paying attention to the teacher?
A: No. The teacher _____
_____ .

12 U11_1
★ 고난도
밑줄 친 ⓐ~ⓓ 중 어법상 어색한 것을 2개 찾아 바르게 고치시오. 6점

A: I ⓐ heard that you ⓑ were cooked carbonara. ⓒ Was it enjoying by all of your guests?
B: Sure. It was so delicious! Everyone wanted ⓓ to eat more.

( ) → _____
( ) → _____

13 U12_3

다음 문장을 각각 주어진 단어를 주어로 시작하는 수동 태 문장으로 바꾸시오. 각 4점

They believe that the grizzly bear is the scariest animal.

*grizzly bear: 회색곰

(1) It _____
_____ .

(2) The grizzly bear _____
_____ .

14 U12_2
Rearrange the given words to make a sentence describing the picture 5점

wig, off, the, the man's, taken, by, monkey, was

→ _____

15 U12_1
✔ 함정
주어진 단어를 바르게 배열하여 수동태 문장을 쓰시오. 5점

by, car, was, to, Guzal, her, the, made, stop, police officer

· 힌트 경찰관은 Guzal이 차를 세우게 했다.

→ _____

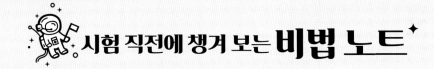

>>> 정답 10쪽

한눈에 쏙! 아래 노트를 보면서 빈칸을 채워 보세요.

1 수동태 형태

① 조동사의 수동태	조동사+1)_____+2)_____
② 진행형의 수동태	3)_____ . +4)b_____ +5)_____ *
③ 완료형의 수동태	6)_____ +7)b_____ +8)_____ **

*be being이 이상한 거 아님! **cf. have done(능동태)

2 5형식 문장의 수동태

① 목적격 보어가 명사/형용사일 때	be+p.p.+명사/형용사
② 목적격 보어가 to부정사일 때	be+p.p.+1)_____ +2)_____
③ 사역동사의 수동태	be+p.p.+3)_____ +4)_____
④ 지각동사의 수동태	be+p.p.+5)_____ +6)_____ be+p.p.+7)_____ ⟩ 둘 다 가능

3 그 외의 수동태

① 동사구의 수동태	be+p.p.+1)_____ +(2)_____ +목적격)*
② that절이 목적어인 경우	They say that he is strange. → It 3)_____ _____ _____ he is strange. → He 4)_____ _____ _____ be strange.

*be looked at by him 이상한 거 아님!

헷갈리지 말자! 초록색으로 표시된 부분을 바르게 고쳐 쓰세요.

1 Half of the rainforest <u>was being destroying</u>.
   ↳

2 The blue shoes <u>had never worn</u> by anybody.
   ↳

3 The kids were seen <u>enter</u> the cave.
   ↳

CHAPTER 07
관계사

UNIT 13   **관계대명사의 역할과 용법**

UNIT 14   **관계부사, 관계사의 생략**

UNIT 15   **복합관계사**

UNIT 13 관계대명사의 역할과 용법

CONCEPT
1 관계대명사의 종류

관계대명사는 앞에 있는 명사나 대명사인 선행사를 수식하는 형용사절을 이끈다.

I know the man. + The man gave flowers to my sister.

→ I know the man who gave flowers to my sister.
　　　　　　선행사　관계대명사　　　　　형용사절

선행사	주격 (+동사)	목적격 (+주어+동사)	소유격
사람	who	who(m) (생략 가능)	whose
사물, 동물	which	which (생략 가능)	whose (= of which)
사람, 사물, 동물	that	that (생략 가능)	
선행사 포함	what	what	

She likes the bag which[that] has a sparkling gem.

The bag which[that] my sister has was made in France.

She likes the bag whose pocket is big.

CONCEPT
2 관계대명사의 용법

A **제한적 용법**: 관계대명사절이 선행사를 뒤에서 수식한다.

He has a daughter who is a doctor. (의사가 아닌 다른 딸이 있는지 알 수 없음)

B **계속적 용법**: 관계대명사절이 선행사를 보충 설명하며, 앞에 comma(,)가 있다.

He has a daughter, who is a doctor. (딸이 하나이고 그 딸이 의사임)

CONCEPT
3 관계대명사 that

that을 쓸 수 없는 경우	that을 주로 쓰는 경우
· 소유격이 없다. · 계속적 용법에는 쓰이지 않는다. · 전치사와 나란히 함께 쓰일 수 없다.	· 선행사에 형용사의 최상급, 서수, the very, the only, the same 등이 있을 때 · 선행사에 all, every, any, no, -thing 등이 있는 경우

There is a student about that (→ whom) we are worried.

She chose the very man that was wearing a blue jacket.

CONCEPT
4 관계대명사 what

the thing(s) which[that](~하는 것)의 뜻으로, 선행사를 포함하고 있으며 명사절을 이끈다.

This is what I want.

You must remember what I said.

GRAMMAR POINT

목적격 관계대명사의 생략
· 목적격으로 쓰인 관계대명사 who(m), which, that은 생략할 수 있다.

관계대명사의 계속적 용법
· 계속적 용법의 관계대명사는 '접속사+대명사'로 바꾸어 쓸 수 있다.

He has a daughter, who is a doctor.

→ He has a daughter, and she is a doctor.

· 계속적 용법의 관계대명사 역시 선행사에 따라 who나 which를 사용하면 된다. 단, that은 계속적 용법으로 사용할 수 없다.

He has a daughter that is a doctor. (○)

He has a daughter, that is a doctor. (×)

· 계속적 용법의 관계대명사가 앞 문장 전체를 가리키는 경우도 있다.

He failed the test, which (= and it) surprised everyone.

(시험에 떨어진 앞 문장 전체 내용을 의미)

선행사가 '사람+동물'인 경우
· 선행사가 사람과 동물이 합쳐진 경우에는 that만 쓴다.

I saw a boy and his dog that were running on the ground.

VOCA　sparkling 반짝이는 | gem 보석 | surprise 놀라게 하다 | the very 바로 그 | the only 유일한 | the same 같은

Let's Check It Out

>>> 정답 10쪽

My score is
/ 15점

A 빈칸에 적절한 관계대명사를 넣으시오. (답이 둘 이상인 경우도 있음) 각 1점

1 I helped the old man _____ you met yesterday.

2 The man _____ brought the pizza is my uncle.

3 The temperature at _____ water freezes is 0°C.

4 I was fond of the man _____ tutored me.

5 Miso showed me _____ she had in her car.

6 This boxed lunch, _____ I bought at a convenience store, tastes great.

B 두 문장을 관계대명사를 이용해서 하나의 문장으로 전환하시오. 각 1점

1 He is the boy. His mother is my English teacher.

→ He is the boy _____ _____ _____ my English teacher.

2 He has a phone. Its functions are simple. (whose)

→ He has a phone _____ _____ _____ _____.

3 She still keeps the thing. I bought the thing for her.

→ She still keeps the thing _____ _____ _____ _____ _____.

→ She still keeps _____ _____ _____ _____ _____.

4 My favorite book is *Harry Potter and the Deathly Hallows*, and I've read it seven times so far.

→ My favorite book is *Harry Potter and the Deathly Hallows*, _____ _____ _____ _____ _____ so far.

C 관계대명사 that과 what 중에서 알맞은 것을 빈칸에 써 넣으시오. 각 1점

1 I helped an old man _____ fell down on the street.

2 She forgot _____ her mother told her.

3 _____ is important is your safety.

4 I really like the raincoat _____ she gave me.

5 That's _____ my brother wants to buy.

VOCA temperature 온도 | freeze 얼다 | be fond of ~을 좋아하다 | tutor 개인 교습을 하다 | boxed lunch (점심) 도시락 | function 기능 | fall down 넘어지다 | safety 안전

1 빈칸에 알맞은 말이 순서새로 짝지어진 것을 고르시오. 3점

> • I have a friend _____ mother is a police officer.
>
> • Do you have a teacher _____ you look up to?

① of which – whose

② whose – whose

③ which – which

④ whose – that

⑤ of which – that

2 Choose the <u>incorrect</u> sentences. 3점

> ⓐ She was the person whom lived with the old lady.
>
> ⓑ I saw the Catholic church that Gaudí built.
>
> ⓒ An orphan is a child who parents are dead.
>
> ⓓ The man whom we met yesterday is a professor.
>
> ⓔ Is this the stone which you are looking for?

① ⓐ, ⓑ   ② ⓐ, ⓒ   ③ ⓑ, ⓒ

④ ⓑ, ⓒ, ⓓ   ⑤ ⓒ, ⓔ

3 Write the proper word for the blank to make the two sentences have the same meaning. 3점

> Many people admire Nelson Mandela, for he fought for the freedom of his countrymen.

→ Many people admire Nelson Mandela, _____ fought for the freedom of his countrymen.

4 Translate the sentence according to the conditions. 6점

> 내가 알고 싶은 것은 그녀의 전화번호이다.
> ----
> · Condition 1   어휘 – want, her phone number
> · Condition 2   9단어로 쓸 것

→ _____

VOCA **look up to** 존경하다 | **Gaudí** 가우디(스페인의 건축가) | **orphan** 고아 | **professor** 교수 | **for** (왜냐하면) ～이므로 | **freedom** 자유 | **countryman** 동포

UNIT 14 관계부사, 관계사의 생략

CONCEPT 1 관계부사 = 전치사 + 관계대명사

관계부사는 시간, 장소, 이유, 방법을 나타내는 선행사를 수식하며, 문장 내에서 '접속사+부사'의 역할을 한다.

This is the place. + We met at the place.

→ This is <u>the place</u> <u>where</u> <u>we met</u>.
       선행사   관계부사   형용사절

	선행사	관계부사	예문
장소	the place	where (= in[on, at] which)	This is the place where we met.
시간	the time	when (= in[on, at] which)	The time when she leaves for America isn't exact.
이유	the reason	why (= for which)	Do you know the reason why he regrets his actions so much?
방법	(the way)	how	He showed me how she danced.

CONCEPT 2 관계사의 생략

관계대명사	목적격 관계대명사	동사의 목적격	There is a meeting (which[that]) we should attend.
		전치사의 목적격	This is the coat of which I am fond. (생략 불가능) This is the coat (which[that]) I am fond of. (생략 가능)
	주격 관계대명사 +be동사		The official language (which is) spoken in India is English.
관계부사	선행사		Tell me (the time) when the flight will depart.
	관계부사		Tell me the time (when) he will arrive.

GRAMMAR POINT

the way와 how

- the way와 how는 함께 쓸 수 없고 둘 중 하나만 써야 한다.

  He showed me <u>how</u> she danced. (○)

  He showed me <u>the way</u> she danced. (○)

  He showed me <u>the way how</u> she danced. (×)

관계부사의 계속적 용법

- 관계부사 앞에 comma(,)가 있다.
- 관계부사 중 where와 when에만 계속적 용법이 쓰인다.
- 관계부사는 '접속사+부사'로 고쳐서 해석한다.

  We went to the zoo, <u>where</u> (= and there) we saw many animals.

  She will return to Seoul on Sunday, <u>when</u> (= and then) I will go to the airport to pick her up.

전치사가 있을 때 관계사의 생략

- 전치사가 관계사절 끝에 있을 때는 관계대명사를 생략할 수 있지만, 전치사와 관계대명사가 붙어 있을 경우에는 생략할 수 없다.

  I remember the place (which[that]) we met <u>in</u>.

  (생략 가능)

  I remember the place <u>in which</u> we met.

  (which 생략할 수 없음)

계속적 용법일 때 생략 여부

- 계속적 용법으로 쓰인 관계사는 생략할 수 없다.

  Michael, <u>whom</u> she loved, became a judge.

  → Michael, she loved, became a judge. (×)

VOCA exact 정확한 | regret 후회하다 | action 행동 | attend 참석하다 | official 공식적인 | language 언어 | flight 비행, 항공편 | depart 출발하다 | judge 판사

Let's Check It Out

>>> 정답 11쪽

A 빈칸에 알맞은 말을 [보기]에서 골라 쓰시오. ^{각 1점}

보기	where	when	how	why

1 Summer is the season _____ everyone likes to travel.

2 She knows the reason _____ he was fired.

3 _____ she treats people is amazing.

4 The place _____ she had dinner with her family specializes in Turkish food.

B 두 문장을 한 문장으로 만들 때 빈칸에 알맞은 말을 쓰시오. ^{각 3점}

1 The university has 30 libraries. + Steve studies at the university.

   (1) The university _____ Steve studies _____ has 30 libraries.

   (2) The university _____ _____ Steve studies has 30 libraries.

   (3) The university _____ Steve studies has 30 libraries.

2 She forgot the day. + She had to register for her classes on the day.

   (1) She forgot the day _____ she had to register for her classes on.

   (2) She forgot the day _____ _____ she had to register for her classes.

   (3) She forgot the day _____ she had to register for her classes.

C 관계대명사가 생략된 부분을 찾아 ∨ 표시하고, 생략된 관계대명사를 쓰시오. ^{각 1점}

1 She will keep the ring she got from her grandmother.   ➡ _____

2 The book he read yesterday was about a missing child.   ➡ _____

3 The man attacked by some strangers is in the hospital now.   ➡ _____

4 The pizza baked in the oven was tasty.   ➡ _____

5 He was the first man I loved.   ➡ _____

VOCA fire 해고하다 | treat 대하다 | amazing 놀라운 | specialize in ~을 전문으로 하다 | Turkish 터키의 | register for ~을 등록하다 | missing 실종된 | attack 공격하다

76

Ready for Exams

>>> 정답 11쪽

My score is

Let's Check It Out _____ / 15점   0~20점 → Level 1 Test
Ready for Exams _____ / 15점 ➡ 21~25점 → Level 2 Test
Total _____ / 30점   26~30점 → Level 3 Test

1   우리말을 영작할 때 적절하지 <u>않은</u> 것을 <u>모두</u> 고르시오. 2점

그들이 살고 있는 집은 수영장이 있다.

① The house where they live in has a pool.
② The house which they live in has a pool.
③ The house that they live in has a pool.
④ The house where they live has a pool.
⑤ The house where they live have a pool.

2   Which correction is right? (2 answers) 2점

ⓐ Have you ever visited a country where French is spoken?
ⓑ Saturday is the day which she goes out with her family.
ⓒThe reason why she got angry was which you hardly understood her.

① ⓐ where → which
② ⓐ where → how
③ ⓑ which → when
④ ⓒ why → which
⑤ ⓒ which → that

3   다음 문장에서 생략 가능한 <u>2단어</u>에 괄호로 표시하시오. 3점

The man who was satisfied with the product ordered another one.

4   다음 조건에 맞게 영작하시오. 각 4점

그는 나에게 그 돈을 번 방법을 말해주었다.

· 조건 1   어휘 – earn the money
· 조건 2   같은 의미의 두 문장을 쓸 것
· 조건 3   과거 시제로 쓸 것

(1) He told me _____.

(2) He told me _____.

VOCA   French 프랑스어 | hardly 거의 ~ 않다 | be satisfied with ~에 만족하다 | product 제품, 상품 | order 주문하다

UNIT 15 복합관계사

1 복합관계대명사: 관계대명사 + -ever

선행사를 포함하는 관계대명사로 명사절 또는 양보의 부사절을 이끌 수 있다.

	명사절	양보의 부사절
whoever(주격)	~하는 사람은 누구든 (= anyone who) Whoever comes is welcome.	누가 ~할지라도 (= no matter who) Whoever may say that, it is not true.
whomever (목적격)	~하는 사람은 누구든지 (= anyone whom) Give it to whomever you like.	누구를[에게] ~할지라도 (= no matter whom) Whomever you may call, he or she will come soon.
whichever (둘 중에서)	~하는 것은 어느 것이든 (= anything that) You may read whichever you like.	어느 것이[것을] ~할지라도 (= no matter which) Whichever you choose, you may have it.
whatever (여러 개 중에서)	~하는 것은 무엇이든 (= anything that) You can drink whatever you want.	무엇이[무엇을] ~할지라도 (= no matter what) Whatever you may say, I will not change my opinion.

2 복합관계부사: 관계부사 + -ever

선행사를 포함하는 관계부사로 시간, 장소, 양보의 부사절을 이끈다.

	시간·장소의 부사절	양보의 부사절
whenever	~할 때는 언제든지 (= at any time when) Whenever I feel depressed, I go shopping.	언제 ~할지라도 (= no matter when) You can come to see me whenever you want.
wherever	~하는 곳은 어디든지 (= at[to] any place where) You may go wherever you like.	어디에서 ~할지라도 (= no matter where) Wherever she is, I'll find her.
however		아무리 ~할지라도 (= no matter how) However rich the man may be, I don't love him.

GRAMMAR POINT

복합관계대명사와 관계대명사

- 복합관계대명사 whatever는 anything that의 의미이고, 관계대명사 what은 the thing which[that]의 의미이다.

  My father gave me whatever I needed.
  → My father gave me anything that I needed.
  (아버지는 내가 원하는 것은 무엇이든지 다 주셨다.)

  My father gave me what I needed.
  → My father gave me the thing that I needed.
  (아버지는 내가 원하는 것을 주셨다.)

whomever/whoever

- 목적격 관계대명사 whom이 who로도 사용되듯이, whomever도 흔히 whoever로 사용된다.

복합관계대명사와 복합관계부사

- 복합관계대명사는 문장에서 명사절, 부사절 둘 다 유도할 수 있다.
  ① 명사절 유도
  Whatever he says is a lie.
  (명사절–주격)
  Give it to whomever (= anyone whom) you meet first.
  (명사절–목적격)
  ② 부사절 유도
  Whatever she wears, she looks wonderful.
  (양보의 부사절)

- 복합관계부사는 강조나 양보의 의미로 부사절만을 이끄는 역할을 한다.
  Come and see me whenever (= at any time when) you want.
  (시간 강조의 부사절)
  Whenever (= No matter when) you come, I will wait for you.
  (양보의 부사절)

VOCA   welcome 환영받는 | opinion 의견 | depressed 우울한, 의기소침한 | go shopping 쇼핑 하러 가다 | lie 거짓말

Let's Check It Out

>>> 정답 11쪽

A [ ]에서 알맞은 것을 고르시오. 각 1점

1 [Which / Whichever] road he may take, he can go to his destination.

2 [Whatever / However] may happen, I am prepared for it.

3 I will give a concert ticket to [whom / whoever] wants it.

4 He will send this invitation to [whichever / whomever] he likes.

B 두 문장의 뜻이 같도록 빈칸에 알맞은 말을 쓰시오. 각 1점

1 Do anything that you want to do.

→ Do _____ you want to do.

2 Anyone who is interested in computers can join our club.

→ _____ is interested in computers can join our club.

3 No matter how hard you may try, you cannot win the race.

→ _____ hard you may try, you cannot win the race.

4 Discrimination is wrong, no matter what the reason is.

→ Discrimination is wrong, _____ the reason is.

5 At any time when I wake up in the morning, I feel energetic.

→ _____ I wake up in the morning, I feel energetic.

C 우리말과 뜻이 같도록 빈칸에 알맞은 말을 쓰시오. 각 1점

1 네가 나의 도움을 필요로 할 때는 언제든지 나는 너를 위해 거기 있을 거야.

→ _____ _____ _____ _____ _____ , I'll
be there for you.

2 그는 어디에 가든지 탈출할 수 있을 것이다.

→ _____ _____ _____ , he will be able to escape.

3 그가 아무리 똑똑할지라도 이 문제를 풀 수는 없다.

→ _____ _____ _____ _____ he is, he can't
solve this problem.

4 너는 이 집에서 네가 원하는 것은 무엇이든 가질 수 있어.

→ You can have _____ _____ _____ _____ in
this house.

VOCA destination 목적지, 도착지 | invitation 초대(장) | discrimination 차별 | reason 이유 | energetic 활력 있는 | escape 탈출하다

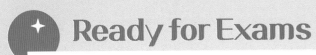

Ready for Exams

>>> 정답 11쪽

My score is

Let's Check It Out _____ / 13점

Ready for Exams _____ / 12점

Total _____ / 25점

0~17점 → Level 1 Test

18~21점 → Level 2 Test

22~25점 → Level 3 Test

---

1 빈칸에 알맞은 것을 고르시오. 2점

> _____ you say, I won't forgive you.

① Whatever ② Whoever ③ Whenever

④ Whomever ⑤ Wherever

2 Which blank needs a different word than the others? 2점

① _____ I feel down, I dance.

② _____ I am sad, I think about the sea.

③ _____ I have a problem, I always talk to my best friend.

④ _____ he goes, his fans will follow him.

⑤ _____ she sees me at school, she smiles.

3 Fill in the blank with one word to make the two sentences have the same meaning. 3점

> No matter what you choose, I don't mind.

→ _____ you choose, I don't mind.

4 그림을 보고 조건에 맞게 우리말을 영작하시오. 5점

> 그가 어디에 나타나든지, 그를 보기 위해 군중
> 들이 모였다.
>
> · 조건1   어휘 – appear, a crowd, gather
> · 조건2   각각의 빈칸에 3단어를 쓸 것
> · 조건3   과거 시제로 쓸 것

→ _____, _____ to see him.

VOCA   forgive 용서하다 | mind 싫어하다, 꺼리다 | appear 나타나다 | crowd 군중 | gather 모이다

80

>>> 정답 11쪽

U13_1

01 Which is the proper word for the blank? 2점

> I know a man _____ IQ (intelligent quotient) is 165.

① who
② which
③ whose
④ what
⑤ that

U13_1+3

02 다음에 대해 바르게 설명한 학생을 <u>모두</u> 고르시오. 4점

★
고난도

> ⓐ I met a friend whom I hadn't seen him for a long time.
> ⓑ I want to know everything that he knows.
> ⓒ The old lady that we saw live alone.
> ⓓ She will tell you who made a mistake.
> ⓔ The man who son is my friend is a doctor.

① 단아: ⓐ him이 없어야 한다.
② 민수: ⓑ that은 which가 되어야 한다.
③ 진하: ⓒ live는 lives가 되어야 알맞다.
④ 효정: ⓓ who가 의미하는 사람은 you이다.
⑤ 지수: ⓔ who는 whose가 되어야 한다.

U13_1+U14_2

03 다음 중 밑줄 친 부분을 <u>생략할 수 없는</u> 것은? 3점

한눈에
쏙

① The man <u>who is</u> working there is my uncle.
② He is the man <u>whom</u> I have met before.
③ This is a chair <u>which was</u> made by Jim.
④ Give me the things <u>which</u> you have now.
⑤ I know a girl <u>whose</u> father is a firefighter.

U13_2

04 밑줄 친 말이 가리키는 것의 성격이 <u>다른</u> 하나는? 2점

① Mike came late, <u>which</u> happens all the time.
② We saw an action movie, <u>which</u> was exciting.
③ He failed the test, <u>which</u> I had expected.
④ Mom agreed to my plan, <u>which</u> encouraged me to work harder.
⑤ Lisa wants to study abroad, <u>which</u> is impossible now.

U13_1

05 Which underlined "that" is grammatically <u>different</u> from the others? 2점

① We can't do anything <u>that</u> we want.
② It is the most interesting movie <u>that</u> I have ever seen.
③ He learned <u>that</u> Jenny could be in trouble.
④ She gave me the money <u>that</u> she owed me.
⑤ All <u>that</u> she has is hope.

U13_3+U14_1

06 주어진 문장을 같은 의미로 바꾸어 쓴 것 중에서 어법에 맞지 <u>않는</u> 것은? 3점

한눈에
쏙

> Donghae is the city where I was born.

① Donghae is the city that I was born in.
② Donghae is the city in which I was born.
③ Donghae is the city which I was born in.
④ Donghae is the city in that I was born.
⑤ Donghae is the city I was born in.

U14_1

07 Whose answer is correct for the blank? 2점

> I watched TV on the day _____ my friend won a gold medal in speed skating.

① 희석: when
② 진구: at which
③ 환기: what
④ 미라: whenever
⑤ 구라: which

U15_1

08 밑줄 친 말과 의미가 같은 것을 고르시오. 2점

> Get <u>anything that</u> you need.

① whatever
② whomever
③ whoever
④ whenever
⑤ wherever

09 다음 문장의 빈칸에 들어갈 알맞은 말은? 2점

> There is a serious disease about _____ we are worried.

① who 　② which

③ whose 　④ what

⑤ that

10 다음 중 빈칸에 들어갈 말이 나머지 넷과 다른 것은? 2점

① I read the book _____ my teacher recommended.

② These are the students _____ Ms. Shin taught last year.

③ He is the boy _____ I was talking about.

④ I remember the man _____ we met at the party.

⑤ This is the park _____ I often take a walk.

11 ★ 고난도

다음 문장에서 생략된 말과 문법적으로 같은 것이 들어 있는 문장은? 4점

> The book my child is reading is written in English.

① Choose one you want to try.

② This is the bag made in France.

③ The man looking for me is my dad.

④ Who is that girl smiling at us?

⑤ I believe everything is going well.

12 다음 문장에 대한 설명으로 바른 것은? 2점

> Whoever comes first gets the best seat.

① Whoever는 Anyone who로 바꾸어 쓸 수 있다.

② comes 는 come으로 써야 한다.

③ gets는 get으로 써야 한다

④ Whoever는 No matter who로 바꾸어 쓸 수 있다.

⑤ Whoever는 '누가~할지라도'라고 해석된다.

13 Which underlined "what" is grammatically <u>different</u> from the given sentence? 2점

> <u>What</u> is most important to learn a foreign language is to become familiar with the language first.

① I can't believe <u>what</u> you said to me.

② This is not <u>what</u> I expected.

③ They want you to do <u>what</u> you have to do.

④ <u>What</u> will the benefits of our new project be?

⑤ <u>What</u> I had for breakfast was oatmeal cereal.

14 밑줄 친 부분과 쓰임이 같은 것을 모두 고르시오. 2점

> Some foods mirror the body parts <u>that</u> they are good for.
>
> *mirror: 보여주다, 반영하다

① She liked the present <u>that</u> I gave her.

② I believe <u>that</u> he will be a good architect.

③ <u>That</u> COVID-19 is highly infectious is true.

④ The thing <u>that</u> she said to us is a lie.

⑤ Isn't it amazing <u>that</u> some foods can treat illnesses?

15 문장에서 생략된 부분을 올바르게 보충해서 쓴 것을 모두 고르시오. 3점

① He is the person we are worried about.

　→ He is the person whom we are worried about.

② Sue was the only guest invited to the event.

　→ Sue was the only guest which was invited to the event.

③ You must remember the thing I said.

　→ You must remember the thing what I said.

④ Tell me the time the class will start.

　→ Tell me the time where the class will start.

⑤ Do you know the reason I am so upset?

　→ Do you know the reason why I am so upset?

16 U13_1

Combine the two sentences into one by using a relative pronoun(관계대명사). 5점

> The boy wants to study politics. His sister is a diplomat.

→ _____

_____

17 U13_2+GP

관계대명사가 사용된 다음 문장을 접속사를 써서 바꾸시오. 4점

> Yesterday, I ran into John, with whom I went to elementary school.

→Yesterday, I ran into John, _____

_____ .

18 U13_1

Complete the translation according to the conditions. 5점

> 그 노인은 상자 옮기는 것을 도와준 소년에게 사탕을 주었다.
>
> ·조건 1 관계사를 포함할 것
> ·조건 2 help동사를 사용할 것

→ The old man gave some candy to _____

_____ him carry the box.

19 U14_GP

다음 대화의 빈칸에 알맞은 말을 쓰시오. 4점

> Do you know what? I lost 5 kilograms in the last three months.
>
> Really? Please tell me _____ you did it.

20 U14_1

Write the common word for the blanks. 4점

> • First, she went to Lima, _____ she received some training to assist the elderly.
> • They didn't have homes, and they didn't know _____ their parents were.

→ _____

21 U15_1

단어 조각을 빈칸 (A)에 바르게 배열하여 문장을 완성하시오. 5점

> A: Do you have any idea about how to spend summer vacation?
> B: No, I don't. No ___(A)___, I'll agree to it.
>
> | what | is | matter | your | idea |

(A) _____

22 U14_2

Translate the sentence according to the conditions. 6점

> 민지(Minji)는 트랙에서 뛰고 있는 남자애한테 홀딱 반해 있어.
>
> ·조건 1 어휘 – have a crush on: ~에게 홀딱 반하다
> ·조건 2 관계대명사를 쓰지 말 것

→ _____

시험 직전에 챙겨 보는 **비법 노트**

>>> 정답 12쪽

한눈에 쏙! 아래 노트를 보면서 빈칸을 채워 보세요.

1 관계사 that

✕ (쓸 수 없는 경우)	○ (주로 쓰는 경우)
• 계속적 용법(콤마 다음에) → ~~that~~ • 전치사 다음에 → ~~that~~	• the ¹⁾v_ _ _ _ , the ²⁾o_ _ _ _ , the ³⁾s_ _ _ _ → (that) • all, every, any, no, -thing → (that)

2 관계사 생략

① (목적격 관·대)+S+V	③ (선행사)+관계부사*
② (¹⁾_____격 관·대+²⁾_____동사)+p.p./-ing	④ 선행사+(³⁾_____)*

*(the way) (how) 둘 중 하나 반드시 생략

3 복합관계사

① whoever	= anyone who 또는 ¹⁾_____ _____ who
② whichever	= anything that 또는 no matter which
③ ²⁾_____	= anything that 또는 no matter what

헷갈리지 말자! 초록색으로 표시된 부분을 바르게 고쳐 쓰세요.

1 History is the subject in _that_ I am interested.

2 This job is _that_ I really want to get.

3 The teacher explained _the way how_ she used Zoom for online classes.

CHAPTER 08
비교 구문

UNIT 16   비교 변화, 원급 이용 비교 구문
UNIT 17   비교급, 최상급 구문

비교 변화, 원급 이용 비교 구문

① 원급, 비교급, 최상급

	단어의 형태	원급 (~한/하게)	비교급 (더 ~한/하게)	최상급 (가장 ~한/하게)
규칙 변화	'자음+y'로 끝나는 경우	easy funny	easier funnier	easiest funniest
	'단모음+단자음'으로 끝나는 경우	big sad	bigger sadder	biggest saddest
	3음절 이상의 형용사/부사	interesting	more interesting	most interesting
	-ful, -ous, -less, -ish로 끝나는 경우 (2음절일 경우도 포함)	careful famous useless foolish	more careful more famous more useless more foolish	most careful most famous most useless most foolish
	-ing, -ed로 끝나는 경우 (분사 형태의 형용사)	boring tired	more boring more tired	most boring most tired

불규칙 변화	good/well – better – best many/much – more – most late – later – latest (시간) far – farther – farthest (거리)	bad/ill – worse – worst little – less – least late – latter – last (순서) far – further – furthest (정도)
	than 대신 to를 쓰는 비교급	**비교, 최상급 관용 표현**
다른 형태 변화	junior to: ~보다 직급[학년]이 낮은 senior to: ~보다 직급[학년]이 높은 superior to: ~보다 우수한[상급의] inferior to: ~보다 열등한[하급의] prefer A to B: B보다 A를 더 좋아하다	would rather A than B: B보다는 차라리 A 하겠다 rather than: ~보다는 오히려 other than: ~을 제외하고 at least: 최소한 ↔ at most: 많아야 at last: 마침내

② 원급을 이용한 구문

A ~ as+원급+as B	A는 B만큼 ~하다	Sneakers are as comfortable as slippers.
A ~ not as[so]+원급+as B (=A ~ less+원급+than B =B ~ 비교급+than A)	A는 B만큼 ~하지 않다 (=B가 A보다 더 ~하다)	The movie is not as funny as the book. (=The movie is less funny than the book. =The book is funnier than the movie.)
as+원급+as possible (=as+원급+as+주어+can[could])	가능한 한 ~한/하게	They will leave as soon as possible. (=They will leave as soon as they can.)
A ~배수사+as+원급+as B (=A ~ 배수사+비교급+than B)	A는 B보다 …배 ~하다	An elephant lives twice as long as a cat. (= An elephat lives two times longer than a cat.)

VOCA　useless 쓸모 없는 | sneakers 운동화 | slippers 슬리퍼 | comfortable 편안한 | possible 가능한

A 빈칸에 알맞은 비교급과 최상급을 쓰시오. 각 1점

	원급	비교급	최상급
1	well		
2	ill		
3	little		
4	far (거리)		
5	far (정도)		
6	late (시간)		
7	late (순서)		

B 우리말과 같은 뜻이 되도록 빈칸에 알맞은 말을 쓰시오. 각 1점

1 그에게 사과하느니 차라리 그를 안 보는 편이 낫겠다.

→ I _____ _____ not see him _____ apologize to him.

2 우리는 더 이상 멀리 가지 않기로 결정했다.

→ We decided not to go any _____.

3 나는 스포츠보다는 오히려 음악을 더 즐긴다.

→ I enjoy music _____ _____ sports.

4 나의 여동생이 회사에서 나보다 직급이 높다.

→ My younger sister is _____ _____ me at my company.

C 두 문장의 뜻이 같도록 빈칸에 알맞은 말을 쓰시오. 각 1점

1 David sings better than Sam.

→ Sam sings _____ _____ David.

2 English is more interesting than math.

→ Math is _____ interesting than English.

→ Math _____ _____ as interesting as English.

3 She slept twice as long as I did.

→ She slept two times _____ _____ I did.

4 We left the house as soon as possible.

→ We left the house as soon as _____ _____.

VOCA apologize 사과하다 | decide 결심하다

Ready for Exams

>>> 정답 12쪽

My score is

Let's Check It Out _____ / 15점   0~20점 → Level 1 Test

Ready for Exams _____ / 15점 → 21~25점 → Level 2 Test

Total _____ / 30점   26~30점 → Level 3 Test

1   빈칸에 알맞은 말이 순서대로 나열된 것은? 3점

> • My puppy is as _____ as my son.
> • Bolt is _____ player on the team.

① lovely – faster

② lovely – the fastest

③ lovelier – the fastest

④ more lovely – the fastest

⑤ more lovely – faster

2   Which set has the proper words for the blanks? (2 answers) 3점

> People think my _____ sister is _____ than me
> because she is much _____ than me.

① older – younger – shorter

② old – young – short

③ older – younger – taller

④ younger – older – taller

⑤ younger – older – shorter

3   Look at the graph and fill in the blanks. 각 3점

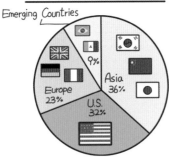

*emerging countries: 신흥 국가

(1) Asians enjoy sci-fi games _____ times _____ than people in

emerging countries.

(2) People in the U.S. don't play sci-fi games _____ _____ as

Asians.

(3) People in the U.S. enjoy sci-fi games _____ _____

Europeans.

VOCA   **sci-fi** 공상 과학의, SF의 | **Asian** 아시아인 | **European** 유럽인

88

비교급, 최상급 구문

1 비교급을 이용한 구문

A ~ 비교급+than B	A는 B보다 더 ~하다	Water is cooler than soda.
The+비교급 ~, the+비교급 … (=As+주어+동사+비교급 ~, 주어+동사+비교급 …)	~하면 할수록, 점점 더 …하다	The higher you climb, the colder it gets. = As you climb higher, it gets colder.
get/become/grow +비교급+and+비교급	점점 더 ~하게 되다	The Earth is getting hotter and hotter.
the+비교급+of the two	둘 중에 더 ~한	Who is the taller of the two?
(all) the+비교급+because (of)	~ 때문에 그만큼 더 …한	I like him all the better because of his kindness.

2 최상급 구문

one of the+최상급+복수 명사	가장 ~한 … 중 하나	Carbon is one of the most common elements.
the+서수+최상급+단수 명사	~번째로 …한	Japan is the second biggest importer of oil.

3 최상급을 나타내는 표현

A ~ the+최상급+단수 명사	A는 가장 ~한 …이다	Safety is the most important thing.
A ~ 비교급+than any other +단수 명사	A는 어떤 다른 …보다 더 ~하다	Safety is more important than any other thing.
A ~ 비교급+than all (of) the other+복수 명사	A는 다른 모든 …보다 더 ~하다	Safety is more important than all (of) the other things.
No (other)+단수 명사 ~ 비교급 +than A	A보다 더 ~한 것은 없다	No other thing is more important than safety.
No (other)+단수 명사 ~ as[so] +원급+as A	A만큼 ~한 것은 없다	Nothing is as important as safety.
There is nothing+비교급 +than A (= Nothing is+비교급+than A)	A보다 더 ~한 것은 없다	There is nothing more important than safety.

VOCA carbon 탄소 | common 흔한 | element 요소, 원소 | importer 수입국, 수입자 | oil 석유, 기름 | safety 안전 | precious 소중한

Let's Check It Out

A [ ]에서 알맞은 것을 고르시오. 각 1점

1 The more it rains, [the fastest / the faster] people walk.
2 Who is [more brilliant / most brilliant], Daniel or Mike?
3 This is [more boring / the most boring] story that I've ever heard.
4 Which is [the earlier / earlier] of the two?
5 Zoom is one of the most common [tool / tools] for online classes.
6 Is wearing a face mask [the most perfect / the perfect] protection against an infectious disease?

B 두 문장의 뜻이 같도록 빈칸을 채우시오. 각 1점

1 Love is the most precious thing in life.
   → Love is _____ _____ _____ _____ other thing in life.
2 Samsung is the largest company in Korea.
   → _____ _____ company is as large as Samsung in Korea.
3 Is India more diverse than any other country in the world?
   → Is India _____ _____ _____ country in the world?
4 No one is more generous than Ms. Kim is.
   → _____ _____ no one _____ _____ than Ms. Kim.

C 우리말과 같은 뜻이 되도록 괄호 안의 단어를 이용하여 빈칸을 채우시오. (필요하면 단어의 형태를 바꿀 것) 각 1점

1 그녀는 인기가 높아질수록 더 오만해졌다. (arrogant)
   → _____ _____ popular she was, _____ _____ _____ she became.
2 그녀는 그 일이 점점 더 매력 없다고 느꼈다. (little)
   → She found the job _____ _____ _____ attractive.
3 나는 그녀가 똑똑하기 때문에 더욱 좋다. (all, good)
   → I like her _____ _____ _____ _____ she is smart.

VOCA brilliant 총명한 | common 흔한 | tool 도구 | protection 보호 | infectious disease 전염병 | precious 소중한 | diverse 다양한, 다채로운 | generous 관대한 | arrogant 오만한 | attractive 매력적인

1   주어진 문장과 의미가 <u>다른</u> 것을 고르시오. 2점

> The elephant is the largest animal on land.

① The elephant isn't as large as any other animal on land.
② No other animal on land is larger than the elephant.
③ The elephant is larger than all of the other animals on land.
④ The elephant is larger than any other animal on land.
⑤ No other animal on land is as large as the elephant.

2   How many sentences are grammatically <u>incorrect</u>? 2점

> ⓐ Ronaldo is the most diligent student in us.
> ⓑ He is more playful of the two boys.
> ⓒ She has one of the oldest coin in the world.
> ⓓ The more you practice, the easier it will be.
> ⓔ My heart beat stronger and stronger.

① 1개   ② 2개   ③ 3개
④ 4개   ⑤ 5개

3   Look at the picture and fill in the blanks with the proper words. Use the given words. 각 4점

(1) _____ _____ we go to the bottom of the sea,
_____ _____ it becomes. (low, dark)

(2) _____ we go _____ to the bottom of the sea, it
becomes _____. (low, dark)

VOCA   diligent 부지런한, 근면한 | playful 장난기 많은 | beat (−beat−beat) 뛰다 | bottom 바닥

CHAPTER 08
Review Test
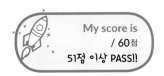
My score is
/ 60점
51점 이상 PASS!!

>>> 정답 13쪽

U16_2

01 두 문장의 뜻이 같도록 할 때 빈칸에 알맞은 것은? 2점

> The novel is not as sad as I expected.
> = The novel is _____ I expected.

① twice as sad as
② sadder than
③ less sad than
④ so sad as
⑤ as sad as

U16_1

02 각 빈칸에 알맞은 말로 짝지어진 것은? 2점

> She _____ going to the movies _____ watching TV.

① rather – than
② would rather – to
③ prefers – than
④ prefers – to
⑤ would rather – than

U17_2

03 Who finds the error and corrects it properly? 2점

> Australia is sixth largest country in the world.

① 서연: country → countries
② 지호: sixth → six
③ 세미: largest → the most large
④ 명수: sixth → the sixth
⑤ 주혜: 틀린 것이 없다.

U17_3

04 다음 문장 중 의미가 다른 하나는? 3점

① The Pacific is the largest ocean.
② The Pacific is larger than any other ocean.
③ No ocean is as large as the Pacific.
④ No ocean is larger than the Pacific.
⑤ The Pacific is as large as the other oceans.

U16_2

05 Which ones are grammatically incorrect? 4점

고난도

> ⓐ She reads books as many as I do.
> ⓑ He studies as twice hard as you.
> ⓒ I saved as much money as I could.

① ⓐ, ⓑ
② ⓐ
③ ⓑ
④ ⓐ, ⓒ
⑤ ⓑ, ⓒ

U17_1

06 빈칸에 가장 알맞은 것은? 2점

> The more money you make, _____.

① more you spend
② you spend more
③ the more you spend
④ you spend the more
⑤ the spend you more

U16_1+2

07 남학생들의 운동 선호도를 나타낸 다음 차트를 잘못 분석한 것은? 3점

한눈에 쏙

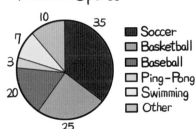

Favorite Sports

Soccer / Basketball / Baseball / Ping-Pong / Swimming / Other

① Boys like soccer five times more than swimming.
② Boys like basketball more than baseball.
③ Baseball is the second favorite sport.
④ Boys like ping-pong less than swimming.
⑤ Boys don't like baseball as much as soccer.

U16_2

08 Read the dialog and write a complete sentence according to the conditions. 4점

> A: Who is more intelligent, Philip or Jack?
>
> B: Jack is more intelligent.
>
> ·Condition 1   Compare Philip and Jack.
> ·Condition 2   Use the word "as."
> ·Condition 3   Write a negative sentence in 6 words.

→ _____

U17_2

09 주어진 단어를 사용해서 다음 우리말을 영작하시오. 5점

함정

> Jenny는 우리 반에서 가장 뛰어난 학생 중 하나이다.
>
> ·단어   brilliant, my class

→ _____

_____

U16_2

10 다음은 문방구에서 묶어 파는 상품들이다. 그림에 맞게 주어진 조건에 따라 두 상품의 가격을 비교하시오. 각 4점

한눈에
쏙

구슬 10개 1000원   연필 2자루 1000원

> ·조건 1   배수사가 사용된 같은 의미의 두 문장을 쓸 것
> ·조건 2   (1)에는 as를 쓸 것
> ·조건 3   (2)에는 than을 쓸 것

(1) A pencil is _____

_____ a bead.

(2) A pencil is _____

_____ a bead.

U17_1

11 빈칸에 알맞은 글자와 단어를 넣어 영작을 완성하시오.

6점

★
고난도

> 나는 룸메이트와의 관계가 점점 더 멀어지고 있다고 느꼈다.

→ I felt that the relationship with my roommate

was g __ __ __ __ __ __ __

_____ distant.

U17_1

12 다음 문장과 같은 의미의 문장을 완성하시오. 4점

> As you practice taekwondo more, you will get better at it.

→ The more _____ ,

_____ .

[13~15] 다음 표를 보고 물음에 답하시오.

	Mt. Baekdu	Mt. Halla	Mt. Jiri
Height	2,744m	1,950m	1,915m
Scenery	★★★	★★★★★	★★
Difficulty	★★★★★	★★★	★

U17_2

13 위의 표에 알맞게 주어진 단어로 문장을 완성하시오. 4점

→ Mt. Baekdu is _____ _____

of all three _____ . (high, mountain).

U16_1+U17_1

14 Read the dialog and fill in blank (A) by using the given words. 5점

함정

> A: Which mountain is more beautiful, Mt. Halla or Mt. Jiri?
>
> B: According to this information, Mt. Halla is ___(A)___ .
>
> ·단어   beautiful, of, two

(A) _____

U17_3

15 표의 내용에 따라 조건에 맞게 문장을 완성하시오. 6점

★
고난도

> ·조건 1   백두산 등반의 어려움에 대해 쓸 것
> ·조건 2   비교급을 이용하여 최상급의 의미를 표현할 것
> ·조건 3   어휘 – difficult, any, no, to, climb

(1) Mt. Baekdu _____

_____ .

(2) _____

_____ than Mt. Baekdu.

시험 직전에 챙겨 보는 **비법 노트**

>>> 정답 13쪽

한눈에 쏙! 아래 노트를 보면서 빈칸을 채워 보세요.

1 원급, 비교급, 최상급

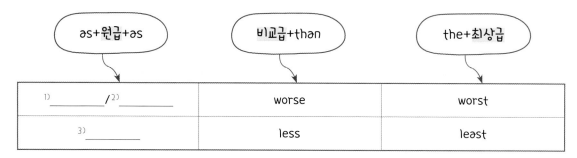

as+원급+as	비교급+than	the+최상급
1) _____ / 2) _____	worse	worst
3) _____	less	least

2 than 대신 to를 쓰는 비교급

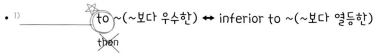

- 1) _____ ~ (~보다 우수한) ↔ inferior to ~ (~보다 열등한)

- prefer A 2) _____ B (B보다 A를 더 좋아하다)

3 중요 비교급 · 최상급 구문

the+비교급 ~, the+비교급 …	1) _____	
부정 주어+as+2) _____ +as ~	~만큼 …한 것은 없다	
부정 주어+3) _____ +4) _____	~보다 더 …한 것은 없다	= 최상급
비교급+than 5) _____ +단수 명사	다른 모든 ~보다 더 …하다	

헷갈리지 말자! 초록색으로 표시된 부분을 바르게 고쳐 쓰세요.

1 December is last month of the year.

2 Some people think modern music is inferior than the music from the past.

3 More you have, the more you want.

CHAPTER 09
분사

UNIT 18 **분사**
UNIT 19 **분사구문**

UNIT 18 분사

CONCEPT 1 현재분사와 과거분사

분사는 동사의 성질을 가지면서 형용사의 역할을 한다.

	형태	의미	역할
현재분사	동사원형+-ing	• 능동: ~하는, ~하게 하는 • 진행: ~하고 있는	• 형용사 역할: 명사 수식, 보어 • 진행형에 쓰임
과거분사	동사원형+-ed (불규칙 동사의 경우: 동사의 과거분사형)	• 수동: ~되어진/지는 • 완료: ~되어 있는	• 형용사 역할: 명사 수식, 보어 • 완료형, 수동태에 쓰임

Look at the sleeping panda.
There was a broken glass.
Sarah is loved by everybody.

My sister is making a model plane.
I have studied English for five years.

CONCEPT 2 감정을 나타내는 분사

분사가 형용사화된 것으로 감정을 나타낸다.

boring 지루하게 하는 bored 지루해하는	exciting 흥분시키는 excited 흥분한	tiring 피곤하게 하는 tired 피곤한
surprising 놀라게 하는 surprised 놀란	shocking 충격을 주는 shocked 충격을 받은	disappointing 실망시키는 disappointed 실망한
satisfying 만족시키는 satisfied 만족한	confusing 혼란시키는 confused 혼란스러운	embarrassing 당황하게 하는 embarrassed 당황한
pleasing 기쁘게 하는 pleased 기쁜	annoying 짜증 나게 하는 annoyed 짜증 난	interesting 관심을 갖게 하는 interested 관심 있는
amazing 놀라운 amazed 놀란	frustrating 좌절시키는 frustrated 좌절한	depressing 우울하게 하는 depressed 우울한
fascinating 매혹적인 fascinated 매혹된	moving 감동적인 moved 감동 받은	frightening 무섭게 하는 frightened 무서워하는

CONCEPT 3 현재분사와 동명사

현재분사	동명사
형용사적 성질: 명사 수식, 보어 역할, 진행형	명사적 성질: 주어, 목적어, 보어 역할

I don't like the barking dog. (현재분사)

I enjoy playing the guitar in the garden. (동명사)

GRAMMAR POINT

분사가 명사 뒤에 오는 경우

• 분사의 뒤에 목적어나 수식어구가 있을 때는 명사 뒤에 위치하여 그 명사를 수식한다. 분사와 그 뒤에 오는 말을 합쳐서 분사구라고 한다.

The woman <u>wearing glasses</u> is my mom.

• 이때 명사와 분사구 사이에 '주격 관계대명사+be동사'가 생략된 것으로 볼 수 있다.

The woman <u>(who is) wearing glasses</u> is my mom.

현재분사와 과거분사의 구별

• 현재분사는 '~한 감정을 느끼게 하는' 의 의미이고, 과거분사는 '~한 감정을 느끼는'의 의미이다.

His work satisfied his boss.
→ His work was satisfying.
→ His boss was satisfied with his work.

VOCA model plane 모형 비행기 | break (–broke–broken) 깨다, 깨지다 | bark 짖다

Let's Check It Out

>>> 정답 14쪽

A [ ]에서 알맞은 것을 고르시오. 각 1점

1 Look at the [exciting / excited] audience.
2 Who is the [dancing / danced] girl?
3 There is a bird [singing / sung] in the tree.
4 We should recycle [using / used] paper.
5 What languages are [speaking / spoken] in Switzerland?

B 괄호 안의 말을 빈칸에 알맞은 형태로 쓰시오. 각 1점

1 Jesse is _____ in reading novels. (interest)
2 The _____ girl is my little sister. (cry)
3 The movie is _____. (excite)
4 He was very _____ with the game. (disappoint)
5 There are many children _____ in line. (wait)

C 밑줄 친 부분이 현재분사이면 '현', 동명사이면 '동'으로 표시하시오. 각 1점

1 We have to take the bus <u>coming</u> over there.   → _____
2 She is good at <u>taking</u> pictures.   → _____
3 I heard him <u>singing</u> a song.   → _____
4 <u>Helping</u> others is not that difficult.   → _____
5 He is <u>climbing</u> the tree.   → _____

D 우리말에 맞도록 괄호 안의 단어를 빈칸에 알맞은 형태로 쓰시오. 각 1점

1 놀라운 장면(surprise)   → a _____ scene
2 놀란 아기(surprise)   → a _____ baby
3 지루한 수업(bore)   → a _____ class
4 지루해하는 학생(bore)   → a _____ student
5 감동적인 영화(move)   → a _____ movie
6 감동 받은 관객(move)   → a _____ audience
7 침낭(sleep)   → a _____ bag
8 자고 있는 아이(sleep)   → a _____ kid

VOCA audience 관객, 청중 | recycle 재활용하다 | language 언어 | novel 소설 | be good at ~을 잘하다

1 괄호 안의 동사를 각 빈칸에 알맞게 쓴 것으로 짝지어진 것은? 2점

> She felt so sad seeing the _____ (destroy) houses and the
> _____ (cry) people.

① destroying – crying
② destroying – cried
③ destroyed – cry
④ destroyed – crying
⑤ destroyed – cried

2 Who finds the error and corrects it properly? 3점

> An elderly man was walking on the beach under the burn sun.

① 창수: was → were
② 승준: was walking → walking
③ 보라: on the beach → of the beach
④ 소희: under → from
⑤ 준수: burn → burning

3 밑줄 친 부분의 쓰임이 나머지와 <u>다른</u> 하나는? 2점

① There is a boy <u>watering</u> the flowers in the garden.
② My dad's nickname is "<u>cooking</u> mom."
③ Look! Someone is <u>standing</u> over there.
④ Sally drew a cow <u>grazing</u> in the pasture.
⑤ <u>Doing</u> our best is the most important thing.

4 Write a sentence describing the picture according to the conditions. 5점

> ·조건 1 주어는 He로 할 것
> ·조건 2 시제는 과거로 할 것
> ·조건 3 동사 surprise와 명사 scene을 활용할 것
> ·조건 4 총 6단어로 구성할 것

→ _____

VOCA destroy 파괴하다 | elderly 나이가 지긋한 | water 물을 주다 | nickname 별명 | graze (풀 등을) 뜯어먹다 | pasture 목장 | do one's best 최선을 다하다 | scene 장면

UNIT 19 분사구문

CONCEPT 1 분사구문의 의미와 전환법

분사구문이란 분사를 이용하여 부사절을 부사구로 바꾼 구문을 말한다.

접속사	주로 삭제
주어	주절의 주어와 같을 때 → 삭제 / 주절의 주어와 다를 때 → 남김
동사	-ing(문두의 Being은 생략 가능)

~~Because~~ <u>they</u> had nothing to do, <u>they</u> felt bored.

→ Having nothing to do, they felt bored.

CONCEPT 2 분사구문의 용법

시간	When I arrived at the station, I called him to pick me up. → Arriving at the station, I called him to pick me up.
이유	Because I didn't know where I was, I asked a police officer. → Not knowing where I was, I asked a police officer.
조건	If you are left behind, you should let me know. → (Being) Left behind, you should let me know.
양보	Although Jane had a bad cold, her boss made her work harder. → Jane having a bad cold, her boss made her work harder.
동시 동작	Sakahi read a Korean novel while he was listening to K-pop. → Listening to K-pop, Sakahi read a Korean novel.
연속 동작	The bellman opened the door and delivered my luggage. → The bellman opened the door, delivering my luggage.

CONCEPT 3 독립분사구문과 비인칭 독립분사구문

독립분사구문	주어+분사 ~	분사구문의 주어 ≠ 주절의 주어
비인칭 독립분사구문	(주어 생략)+분사 ~	분사구문의 주어가 일반인인 경우

It being fine, we wanted to have a class outside. (독립분사구문)

Judging from the rumor, the lady may be his girlfriend. (비인칭 독립분사구문)

CONCEPT 4 with + 목적어 + 분사

with+목적어+	현재분사	목적어와 능동 관계	~이 …한 채로
	과거분사	목적어와 수동 관계	~이 …된 채로

She went shopping with her husband accompanying her. (목적어와 능동 관계)

Elena sat down on the bench with her arms folded. (목적어와 수동 관계)

GRAMMAR POINT

분사구문의 부정
- 분사구문의 부정은 'not[never]+분사'로 한다

-ed 분사구문
- 앞에 being이 생략된 것으로 주절과의 관계가 수동이다.

  <u>Excited</u> about the win, they jumped and shouted.

  (they와 excite의 관계가 수동)

분사구문의 시제
- 단순 분사구문(동사원형+-ing): 주절과 같은 시제

  <u>Feeling</u> too hot, he didn't want to take a walk.

  → Because he <u>felt</u> too hot, he <u>didn't</u> want to take a walk.

- 완료 분사구문(having+p.p.): 주절보다 앞선 시제

  <u>Having left</u> my phone at home, I couldn't contact you.

  → Because I <u>had left</u> my phone at home, I <u>couldn't</u> contact you.

having been의 생략
- 완료 분사구문에서 having been도 생략 가능하다.

  Though she was warned the last time, she still drives fast.

  → (Having been) Warned the last time, she still drives fast.

주요 비인칭 독립분사구문
- generally speaking (일반적으로 말해서)
- frankly speaking (솔직히 말하면)
- roughly speaking (대강 말하자면)
- strictly speaking (엄격히 말해서)
- judging from (~로 판단하건대)
- considering (that) (~을 고려하면)

VOCA   K-pop 가요 | bellman (호텔의) 짐꾼 | accompany 동행하다 | fold 접다, 포개다

A 분사구문을 이용해 문장을 전환할 때 빈칸에 알맞은 말을 쓰시오. ^{각 1점}

1 When he saw the tiger, he felt scared.

→ _____ the tiger, he felt scared.

2 As I didn't feel hungry, I skipped breakfast.

→ _____ _____ hungry, I skipped breakfast.

3 Tina and Rick were sitting on the couch as they watched TV.

→ _____ _____ , Tina and Rick were sitting on the couch.

4 As my father was busy washing his car, I did the dishes.

→ _____ _____ _____ _____ washing his car, I

did the dishes.

B [ ]에서 알맞은 것을 고르시오. ^{각 1점}

1 [Feeling / Felt] tired, she went to bed early.

2 [Not living / Living not] with his family, he has to take care of himself.

3 [Having stayed / Staying] up all night, the secretary kept on yawning.

4 It [is / being] fine tomorrow, we'll ride on a yacht.

5 She walked away with tears [run / running] down her face.

C 밑줄 친 부분이 어법상 어색하면 바르게 고치시오. ^{각 1점}

1 <u>Eaten</u> a lot of sweets, you'll put on some weight.

→ _____

2 My roommate <u>having</u> the key, I couldn't get into the room.

→ _____

3 They welcomed us, <u>and serving</u> warm milk.

→ _____

4 <u>Being born</u> in Quebec, he can speak French.

→ _____

VOCA scared 겁먹은 | skip 거르다 | do the dishes 설거지하다 | yawn 하품하다 | sweet 단것 | put on weight 살이 찌다 | Quebec 퀘벡(캐나다에서 프랑스어를 쓰는 지역)

My score is

Let's Check It Out _____ / 13점   0~17점 → Level 1 Test
Ready for Exams _____ / 12점 → 18~21점 → Level 2 Test
Total _____ / 25점   22~25점 → Level 3 Test

1 밑줄 친 부분을 분사구문으로 바꾸어 쓴 것으로 알맞은 것은? 3점

> As I work near her office, I often see her.

① Being work near her office

② Working near her office

③ Worked near her office

④ Having worked near her office

⑤ As I working near her office

2 Who analyzes the underlined part correctly? 3점

> Finding by the dog, Kate was taken to a nearby hospital.

① 김나리A: Kate가 주어니까 Finding은 맞는 표현이야.

② 김나리B: If she was found ~으로 바꿔 쓸 수 있어.

③ 강태풍: 개가 먼저 발견한 거니까 Having finding ~으로 써야 해.

④ 맹세코: Having been은 생략 가능하니까 Found ~로 써야 해.

⑤ 구라임: 의미상 Was found ~라고 써야 해.

3 Look at the picture and complete the sentence according to the conditions. 각 3점

· Condition 1   (A)는 과거 진행형으로 쓸 것
· Condition 2   (B)는 '그들의 눈을 감은 채'라는 뜻이 되도록 하고 with를 사용할 것
· Condition 3   어휘 – dance, their eyes, close

→ Grandma and Grandpa (A) _____ to the music

  (B) _____.

VOCA   nearby 근처의

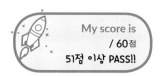

>>> 정답 14쪽

01 U18_1
Which is suitable for the blank? 2점

> I have too much homework. Look at my schedule _____ with homework.

① fill   ② filling
③ be filling   ④ filled
⑤ have filled

02 U18_1+GP
다음 우리말 문장을 올바르게 영작한 것은? 2점

> 그의 뒤에 서 있는 소녀를 봐.

① Look at the girl who is stood behind him.
② Look at the girl who is standing behind him.
③ Look at the girl who standing behind him.
④ Look at the girl stood behind him.
⑤ Look at the girl that is stood behind him.

03 U18_2+GP
다음 중 어법상 어색한 문장은? 2점

① The piano concert was boring.
② Today's episode was very interesting.
③ I was very shocking at the news.
④ He was embarrassed by her behavior.
⑤ The magic show was amazing.

04 U19_1+GP
밑줄 친 부분의 의미 풀이가 알맞지 <u>않은</u> 것은? 3점

한눈에 쏙

① <u>The doll being torn</u>, she still loves having it.
  = Though the doll is torn
② <u>Not having a car</u>, he had to walk to work.
  = Since he didn't have a car
③ <u>Left alone at home</u>, you'll be bored to death.
  = If you left alone at home
④ <u>Walking down the street</u>, I met a friend of yours.
  = While I was walking down the street
⑤ She asked my number, <u>calling me on the spot</u>.
  = and she called me on the spot

05 U18_3
밑줄 친 부분의 쓰임이 나머지와 <u>다른</u> 하나는? 2점

① They enjoyed <u>meeting</u> new people.
② You're <u>playing</u> your music too loudly.
③ I like <u>keeping</u> a diary in English.
④ <u>Finishing</u> the race is his goal.
⑤ <u>Becoming</u> a famous singer is my dream.

06 U19_1+2+GP
빈칸에 들어갈 말을 바르게 이해한 학생은? 2점

한눈에 쏙

> _____ in the town almost half a century, the old lady knows everyone there.

① 진수: 내용상 '~했을지라도'로 해석할 수 있어.
② 수민: 앞 문장이 앞선 시제이므로 Lived로 써야 해.
③ 민서: 분사구문이니까 Living이 답이야.
④ 서일: 앞선 시제이므로 Having lived로 써야 해.
⑤ 일미: Since she had lived로 써도 맞아.

07 U19_3
밑줄 친 우리말을 영어로 바르게 옮긴 것은? 2점

> <u>그녀의 나이를 고려하면</u>, she swims very fast.

① Consider her age
② If she considers her age
③ Her age considering
④ Considering her age
⑤ Her age was considered

08 U19_1+3
How many are grammatically correct? 4점

고난도

> ⓐ Having no friends, I don't feel lonely.
> ⓑ It cold, I had to stay home all day long.
> ⓒ Arrived just before the movie, I could go in.
> ⓓ Riding her bike, Anna scraped her knee.
> ⓔ Disappointing by his reaction, she decided not to see him.
> ⓕ Having studied for five hours, I felt tired.

① one   ② two
③ three   ④ four
⑤ five

U18_1

09 Rewrite the sentence by correcting the error. 4점

> Look at the window breaking by the ball.

→ _____

U18_GP

10 우리말과 같은 의미가 되도록 단어 조각을 배열하시오. 4점

> 4시에 시작하는 그 공연에 늦지 마라.
>
> | Don't | be | at 4 | | the concert |
> | for | starting | late | | |

→ _____

U18_2+GP

11 조건에 맞게 우리말을 영작하시오. 5점

★ 고난도

> 나는 그의 행동에 약간 실망했다.
>
> ·조건 1 rather를 이용할 것
> ·조건 2 I를 주어로 할 것
> ·조건 3 7단어로 완성할 것

→ _____

U18_1+GP

12 Look at the picture and complete the sentence. 4점

✔ 함정

·단어 smile, draw

→ There is a _____ _____
_____ on the cup.

U19_GP

13 [보기]와 같이 –ing 형태를 써서 바꾸시오. 4점

> [보기] While he was singing loudly, he went out.
>
> → Singing loudly, he went out.
>
> As I don't have time, I can't help you.

→ _____, I can't help you.

U19_1

14 Rearrange the given words to make a sentence according to the conditions. 6점

★ 고난도

> her, window, see, sneaked out, opening, she, to, boyfriend, the
>
> ·Condition 1 분사구문을 먼저 쓸 것
> ·Condition 2 어휘 – sneak out: to leave a place without being seen or heard

→ _____
_____

U19_1+2

15 어법상 어색한 문장을 찾아 바르게 고쳐 쓰시오. 5점

◉ 한눈에 쏙

> ⓐ Surrounded by the sea, the island has a mild climate.
> ⓑ There were neither taxis nor buses, we had to walk back home.

(   ) → _____

_____

U19_4

16 주어진 단어를 이용해서 다음 그림을 설명하는 문장을 완성하시오. 4점

✔ 함정

> follow, her dog, with

→ She was jogging _____ .

U19_GP

17 Find TWO errors and correct them. 5점

✔ 함정

> Having living in her hometown all her life, Maria didn't want moving to another city.

_____ → _____

_____ → _____

한눈에 쏙! 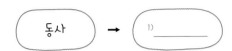아래 노트를 보면서 빈칸을 채워 보세요.

1 분사

동사 → 1) _____

2 현재분사 vs. 과거분사

현재분사(-ing)	~하는	a 1) _ _ _ _ _ _ _ book (지루한 책)
과거분사(-ed)	~하게 된	a 2) _ _ _ _ _ _ student (지루해하는 학생)

3 ☆분사구문

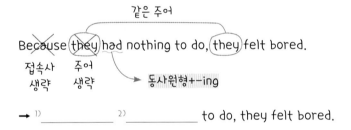

같은 주어

Because (they) had nothing to do, (they) felt bored.
접속사   주어
생략   생략 → 동사원형+-ing

→ 1) _____ 2) _____ to do, they felt bored.

헷갈리지 말자! 초록색으로 표시된 부분을 바르게 고쳐 쓰세요.

1 The man worn a beard is my dad.
　　　　　└→

2 Look at the cow that is grazed in the pasture.
　　　　　　　　　　　　　└→

3 Surprising by the news, we couldn't say anything.
　└→

4 Seen the tragic ending of the movie, I felt depressing.
　└→　　　　　　　　　　　　　　　　　　　└→

5 Elena sat down on the bench with her arms folding.
　　　　　　　　　　　　　　　　　　　　　└→

CHAPTER 10
접속사

UNIT 20   등위 접속사, 상관 접속사, 종속 접속사

UNIT 21   종속 접속사

UNIT 20 등위 접속사, 상관 접속사, 종속 접속사

1 등위 접속사

대등한 형태의 단어와 단어, 구와 구, 절과 절을 연결해 주는 역할을 한다.

A and B	A 그리고 B	My joints were stiff and sore. (나의 관절이 뻣뻣하고 쑤셨다.)
A but B	A 그러나 B	Many are invited, but few are chosen. (초대되는 자는 많으나 선택되는 자는 적다.)
A or B	A 또는 B	Would it be better to buy or to rent a house? (집을 사는 게 좋을까 아니면 임대하는 게 나을까?)

2 상관 접속사

서로 짝을 이루면서 대등한 관계로 두 개의 문장 요소를 연결한다. 등위 접속사와 마찬가지로 병렬 구조를 이룬다.

both A and B	A와 B 둘 다	Both my mom and I are models.
not A but B	A가 아니라 B	Not the result but the process counts.
either A or B	A와 B 둘 중 하나	Either you or she has to go there.
neither A nor B	A도 B도 아닌	Neither she nor I have any idea about it.
not only A but (also) B =B as well as A	A뿐만 아니라 B도	Not only you but also he was wrong. = He as well as you was wrong.

3 명사절을 이끄는 종속 접속사

절 전체를 명사(주어, 목적어, 보어)로 만드는 역할을 한다. that절이나 whether절이 주어로 사용될 때는 대개 가주어 It을 사용하는 문장으로 바꾼다.

that	~라는 것, ~라고	That he is alive is certain. (주절) → It is certain that he is alive. I think (that) he is a great hero. (목적절) His strength is that he is honest. (보어절)
whether (목적절일 때는 if도 가능)	~인지 (아닌지)	Whether the vaccine is safe (or not) is important. (주절) → It is important whether the vaccine is safe (or not). I don't know whether[if] it is true (or not). (목적절) The problem is whether he will come (or not). (보어절)

GRAMMAR POINT

명령문 ~, and/or …

- 「명령문 ~, and …」는 '~해라. 그러면 …할 것이다'라는 의미이다.

  Study hard, and I will buy you a gift.
  → If you study hard, I will buy you a gift.

- 「명령문 ~, or …」는 '~해라. 그렇지 않으면 …할 것이다'라는 의미이다.

  Hurry up, or you will miss the flight.
  → If you don't hurry up, you will miss the flight.
  (= Unless you hurry up, you will miss the flight.)

상관 접속사의 수 일치

- both A and B는 항상 복수로 취급한다.

- not A but B, either A or B, neither A nor B, not only A but also B, B as well as A는 모두 B에 수를 일치시킨다.

병렬 구조

- 등위 접속사나 상관 접속사가 연결하는 두 대상의 문법적 형태는 동일해야 한다.

  The principal is both friendly and generous.

  (그 교장 선생님은 친절하고 관대하시다.)

whether와 if의 차이

- whether 뒤에는 바로 or not을 쓸 수 있지만 if 뒤에는 쓸 수 없다.

- whether는 주절, 목적절, 보어절을 모두 이끌 수 있지만, if는 목적절만 이끌 수 있다.

  If the vaccine is safe (or not) is important. (×)

명사절이 주어일 때 수 일치

- that절이나 whether절이 주어로 쓰일 때는 단수로 취급한다.

  That they take care of poor children is true.

VOCA joint 관절 | stiff 뻣뻣한 | sore 아픈, 따끔거리는 | result 결과 | process 과정 | count 중요하다 | principal 교장 | generous 관대한 | strength 장점, 강점 | vaccine 백신

Let's Check It Out

>>> 정답 15쪽

A [ ]에서 알맞은 것을 고르시오. 각 1점

1 She didn't have breakfast but [lunch / had lunch].
2 She can play the piano [and / but] the cello.
3 Grapes are usually green [and / or] red.
4 I don't like swimming, but I like [to skate / skating].
5 Sit down [and / but] tell me about your school life.

B 어법상 어색한 부분을 찾아 바르게 고치시오. 각 1점

1 You can choose neither pizza or spaghetti.
   _____ ➡ _____

2 Yuri is not only beautiful but also intelligence.
   _____ ➡ _____

3 Jack as well as I love to eat breakfast in bed.
   _____ ➡ _____

4 If he passed the test is what I want to know.
   _____ ➡ _____

C 우리말과 같은 뜻이 되도록 빈칸을 채우시오. 각 1점

1 나는 그녀가 나를 좋아하는지 궁금하다.
   ➡ I wonder _____ she likes me.

2 나는 그가 약속을 지킬지 알 수 없다.
   ➡ I don't know _____ he will keep his promise.

3 그는 돼지고기와 소고기 둘 다 먹지 않는다.
   ➡ He eats _____ pork _____ beef.

4 그들은 경력뿐만 아니라 기술도 요구한다.
   ➡ They demand _____ _____ experience _____
      _____ skills.

5 행복이 작은 것들에 있다는 것은 사실이다.
   ➡ _____ is true _____ happiness lies in small things.

VOCA intelligence 지능 | demand 요구하다 | experience 경험 | skill 기술

Ready for Exams

>>> 정답 15쪽

My score is

Let's Check It Out _____ / 14점	0~17점 → Level 1 Test
Ready for Exams _____ / 11점	18~21점 → Level 2 Test
Total _____ / 25점	22~25점 → Level 3 Test

1 다음 빈칸에 알맞은 것을 고르시오. 2점

_____ my mother _____ my sister is an author.
They are translators.

① Either – nor ② Both – and ③ Neither – nor

④ Neither – or ⑤ Either – or

2 Which sentences are <u>incorrect</u>? 2점

ⓐ Alfredo was neither an architect or a scientist.
ⓑ Both of them are impulsive.
ⓒ Either of them are inappropriate.
ⓓ Both a chair and a table are needed.
ⓔ Not Jake but Tim was late for school yesterday.

① ⓐ ② ⓐ, ⓑ ③ ⓐ, ⓒ

④ ⓑ, ⓒ ⑤ ⓓ, ⓔ

3 Rewrite the sentence by using the given word. Do NOT change the meaning of the sentence. 3점

Not only houses but also a bridge was destroyed. (as)

→ _____

4 그림을 묘사하는 문장을 조건에 맞게 완성하시오. 4점

- 조건 1 어휘 – want, nor, eat snacks, drink yogurt
- 조건 2 필요하면 주어진 어휘의 형태를 변형할 것
- 조건 3 빈칸에 9단어로 쓸 것
- 조건 4 to를 두 번 쓸 것

→ The kid _____.

He wants only a toy robot.

VOCA author 작가 | translator 번역가 | architect 건축가 | impulsive 충동적인 | inappropriate 부적절한 | destroy 파괴하다 | yogurt 요구르트

21 종속 접속사

1 부사절을 이끄는 종속 접속사

시간	when(~할 때), while(~하는 동안에), as(~하면서, ~할 때), since(~한 이래로), after(~한 후에), before(~하기 전에), until(~할 때까지), as soon as(~하자마자)
	When you are not using the charger, pull the plug out.
이유	because, since, as(~하기 때문에)
	I am starving because I didn't have anything to eat.
조건	if(~한다면), unless(~하지 않는다면)
	Unless you have enough money, you can't buy a new car.
양보	though, although, even though(비록 ~일지라도), even if(~한다고 해도)
	Although he was sleepy, he tried to focus on studying. Even if the mission is impossible, we have to keep on going.
목적	so that+주어+can/may/will+동사원형 = in order that+주어+can/may/will+동사원형 = (in order) to+동사원형=so as to(~이 …하도록)
	Blend the ingredients together so that you can make smooth dough.
결과	so+형용사/부사+that+주어+동사(너무 ~해서 …하다) = such (a/an)+명사+that+주어+동사
	She was so tired that she fell asleep quickly. Ben always has such a pleasant smile that everyone likes him.

2 여러 가지 의미로 쓰이는 접속사

since	~한 이래로	Refugees have left the country since the war began.
	~하기 때문에	Since the service was good, I gave an extra large tip.
as	~하면서, ~할 때	The train's whistle blew as it approached the station.
	~함에 따라	As his children grew older, he needed more money.
	~하는 대로	This fish isn't cooked as I like it.
	~하기 때문에	As I was tired, I wanted to rest.
when	명사절(언제)	I want to know when he will leave for London.
	부사절(~할 때)	We were all very pleased when she passed the exam.
if	명사절(~인지)	I wonder if she will accept his proposal.
	부사절(~한다면)	If she accepts his proposal, she will marry him soon.
while	~하는 동안	I continued working while he played all day.
	~하는 한편[반면]	While I enjoy coffee, my mom prefers tea.

GRAMMAR POINT

until과 till

- until은 구어체에서 till로 줄여 쓰기도 한다.

  I won't believe it till I hear it from you.

because와 because of

- because+절(주어+동사)

  I couldn't see anything because it was foggy.

- because of+(동)명사

  I couldn't see anything because of the fog.

부사절과 명사절의 시제 차이

- 시간과 조건의 부사절에서는 현재 시제로 미래를 표현한다.

- 명사절에서는 미래형을 그대로 써야 미래의 뜻을 나타낸다.

  When he comes back, I'll call you. (시간의 부사절)

  I don't know when he will come back. (명사절)

(al)though와 despite[in spite of]

- (al)though+절(주어+동사)

  We enjoyed camping although it rained.

- despite[in spite of]+명사

  We enjoyed camping despite the rain.

so ~ that과 enough to

- so ~ that+주어+can … = ~ enough to… (~할 정도로 충분히 …한)

  Soyeon is so strong that she can carry the desk.

  → Soyeon is strong enough to carry the desk.

- so ~ that+주어+cannot … = too ~ to… (너무 ~해서 …할 수 없는)

  I am so tired that I can't help you.

  → I am too tired to help you.

VOCA charger 충전기 | pull out 빼다 | starve 굶주리다, 굶어 죽다 | mission 임무 | blend 섞다 | ingredient 재료 | dough 반죽 | refugee 난민 | whistle 경적 | approach 접근하다

A **[　]에서 알맞은 것을 고르시오.** 각 1점

1   [If / Although] vegetables are good for me, I don't like them.
2   I had never heard of Super Bowl [before / after] I came to America.
3   [As / Till] I watched the film, I could recall my childhood.
4   I found a ten-dollar bill in my room [while / although] I was cleaning it.
5   I can't check you in [if / unless] you have a passport.
6   She was late [because / because of] the foggy weather.
7   We enjoyed our trip [despite / although] it rained a lot.
8   Lisa is [such a / so] polite student that every teacher likes her.

B **우리말과 같은 뜻이 되도록 빈칸에 알맞은 말을 쓰시오.** 각 1점

1   나는 너무 피곤해서 더 이상 걸을 수 없었다.

→ I was _____ _____ _____ _____ _____
walk anymore.

2   그 질문들은 너무 쉬워서 모든 학생들이 맞게 대답했다.

→ Those questions were _____ easy _____ every student
answered them correctly.

3   중요한 것을 먼저 할 수 있도록 할 일의 목록을 만들어라.

→ Make a to-do list _____ _____ you can do important
things first.

4   또 다시 같은 실수를 하지 않도록 조심해라.

→ Be careful _____ _____ _____ _____ make
the same mistake again.

C **밑줄 친 부분을 우리말로 옮기시오.** 각 1점

1   Morris practiced all day <u>since</u> he wanted to win   →   _____
the contest.

2   We have been friends <u>since</u> we were young.   →   _____

3   I wonder <u>if</u> Tony will visit the fair soon.   →   _____

4   Mom will be upset <u>if</u> you spill milk on the sofa.   →   _____

VOCA   **Super Bowl** 미국 미식축구 결승전 | **recall** 기억해내다, 상기하다 | **childhood** 어린 시절 | **passport** 여권 | **foggy** 안개 낀 | **to-do list** 할 일의 목록 |
fair 박람회 | **spill** 쏟다

Ready for Exams

>>> 정답 16쪽

1 다음 두 빈칸에 공통으로 알맞은 것은? 2점

• You can make an enormous profit _____ you accept my plan.
• I'm not sure _____ the car consumes lots of gas.

① when   ② if   ③ whether
④ as   ⑤ although

2 영영사전에 나온 as의 다섯 가지 의미 중에서 [보기]의 밑줄 친 as에 해당하는 것은? 2점

보기   • I hummed <u>as</u> I walked down the street.
       • The phone rang <u>as</u> we were leaving the house.

① to the same degree or quantity that
   (The situation is not as bad <u>as</u> you see.)
② at the same time that; while
   (I slipped on the ice <u>as</u> I was running home.)
③ for the reason that; because
   (I went to bed early <u>as</u> I was exhausted.)
④ in the same manner or way that
   (Do in Rome <u>as</u> the Romans do.)
⑤ though
   (Great <u>as</u> the author was, he proved to be a bad person.)

3 Complete the translation according to the conditions. 5점

그 책이 너무 재미있어서 나는 그것을 읽는 것을 멈출 수가 없었다.

·Condition 1   과거 시제로 쓸 것
·Condition 2   어휘 – interesting, stop reading
·Condition 3   빈칸에 9단어로 쓸 것

➡ The book _____

_____ .

VOCA   enormous 거대한 | profit 이익 | consume 소비하다 | hum 콧노래를 부르다 | degree 정도 | quantity 양 | exhaust 지치게 하다 |
author 작가

UNIT **21**   111

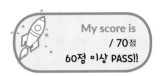

>>> 정답 16쪽

U20_2+U21_1

01 다음 중 어느 빈칸에도 들어갈 수 <u>없는</u> 것은? 3점

> • Neither she _____ he is not happy.
> • I will buy either apples _____ oranges.
> • She ran away as soon _____ she saw me.
> • He is not only an artist _____ also a scientist.

① or   ② as   ③ and
④ but   ⑤ nor

U21_1

02 Choose the proper word for the blank. 2점

> I'll love him _____ he leaves me.

① if   ② as   ③ when
④ even if   ⑤ because

U21_2

03 밑줄 친 if의 의미가 나머지와 <u>다른</u> 것은? 2점

① Is it okay if I ride your bike?
② Bill says he can get all A's if he wants to.
③ If you let me play now, I'll study all night.
④ Do you mind if I go to the movies tonight?
⑤ I'm not sure if you can do that.

U21_GP

04 How many are grammatically correct? 4점

★ 고난도

> ⓐ Juliet should give up playing soccer before her injury gets worse.
> ⓑ I don't know when she will marry him.
> ⓒ He will buy a convertible when he will save enough money.
> ⓓ Stay away from him if he approaches you.
> ⓔ He will change his mind when you're gone.

① one   ② two   ③ three
④ four   ⑤ five

U21_1+2

05 이유를 나타내는 문장이 <u>아닌</u> 것을 고르시오. 2점

① As she was mad at him, she said nothing.
② She failed the test because she made a few mistakes.
③ Since it was raining all day, we stayed home.
④ Since I was a baby, I have always loved animals.
⑤ We tried to be quiet since she was studying.

U21_1+2

06 Which is NOT proper for the blank? 2점

> _____ the flower is beautiful, it has many thorns.

① Though   ② Although
③ As if   ④ Even though
⑤ While

U20_3+U21_1+2

07 밑줄 친 부분의 쓰임이 <u>다른</u> 하나는? 3점

 한눈에 쏙

① Cook slowly <u>until the noodles are tender</u>.
② We need to know <u>if the tour is safe</u>.
③ It has been a long time <u>since I met her</u>.
④ Don't count your chickens <u>until they are hatched</u>.
⑤ Turn off the lights <u>when you leave the room</u>.

U21_2

08 밑줄 친 As의 뜻이 [보기]와 같은 것은? 3점

 함정

> 보기   <u>As</u> she was not interested, she didn't listen to the lecture.

① <u>As</u> I didn't know what to do, I asked for advice.
② <u>As</u> time went by, I felt more comfortable.
③ <u>As</u> he grew up, he felt proud of his family.
④ <u>As</u> the children got bigger, his family needed to get a larger house.
⑤ <u>As</u> he knocked on the door, a giant man came out of the house.

U20_3+U21_GP

09 주어진 단어를 이용하여 우리말을 영작하시오. (9단어) 5점

함정

> 나는 그녀가 이 결정을 좋아할지 모르겠어.
>
> this decision, like, know, don't

→ _____

U20_2+GP

10 조건에 맞게 우리말을 영작하시오. 5점

함정

> 너나 Chris나 TV 보는 것에 관심 있는 것 같지 않아.
>
> ·조건 1 어휘 – neither, seem to 활용
> ·조건 2 '너'를 Chris보다 앞에 쓸 것
> ·조건 3 빈칸에 6단어로 완성할 것

→ _____ be

interested in watching TV.

U20_2

11 조건에 맞게 우리말을 영작한 두 문장을 완성하시오.

★ 고난도

각 5점

> 그녀는 건방질 뿐만 아니라 이기적이다.
>
> ·조건 1 어휘 – arrogant, selfish
> ·조건 2 (1)에는 as를, (2)에는 also를 사용할 것

(1) She is _____ .

(2) She is _____ .

U21_1+GP

12 Write one word that can fill in both blanks. 4점

> • I was _____ exhausted that I couldn't focus on my work.
> • Yuna is saving up _____ that she can travel around the world.

→ _____

U21_1

13 두 빈칸에 공통으로 들어갈 수 있는 말을 쓰시오. 4점

> • _____ conflicts may occur within the family, they are about small things.
> • _____ she lost the final match, she was proud of herself.

→ _____

U21_1

14 조건에 맞게 우리말을 영작한 문장을 완성하시오. 4점

> 그가 다른 사람들에게 귀 기울이지 않는다면, 그는 좋은 관계를 형성할 수 없다.
>
> ·조건 1 어휘 – others, listen to
> ·조건 2 not을 사용하지 말 것

→ _____ , he

cannot build any good relationships.

U21_GP

15 다음 중 어법상 어색한 문장을 찾아 바르게 고치시오. 5점

함정

> ⓐ After I eat dinner, I'm going to do my homework in my room.
> ⓑ Despite she had no experience, we hired her.

( ) _____ → _____

U21_1

16 Look at the picture and translate the sentence according to the conditions. 8점

★ 고난도

> 그녀는 아무도 들어올 수 없도록 문을 잠갔다.
>
> ·Condition 1 과거 시제로 쓸 것
> ·Condition 2 어휘 – so, come in, can, nobody
> ·Condition 3 10단어로 쓸 것

→ _____

_____

U21_GP

17 Find the error and correct it. 4점

> When he will come back tomorrow, I will tell him the truth.

→ _____ → _____

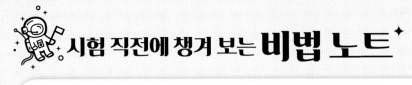
한눈에 쏙! 아래 노트를 보면서 빈칸을 채워 보세요.

1 상관 접속사

• not only A but also B = (B) _____ _____ _____ (A) (A뿐만 아니라 B도)

2 명사절 접속사

• That he is alive is certain. (주절)
  └→ 문장을 명사로 만든다.

3 ~하기 위해

• so that+주어+동사

• in order that+주어+동사

• in order to+동사원형

4 너무 ~해서 …하다

• 1) _____ +형용사/부사+that+주어+동사

• 2) _____ (a/an)+명사+that+주어+동사

헷갈리지 말자! 초록색으로 표시된 부분을 바르게 고쳐 쓰세요.

1 Not only you but also she was correct. = You as well as she were correct.
       └→   └→

2 What he will come is certain.
   └→

3 Blend the ingredients together in order to you can make smooth dough.
                                   └→

4 Jessie has so a happy smile that everyone likes her.
              └→

CHAPTER 11
가정법

UNIT 22   **가정법 과거, 가정법 과거완료**

UNIT 23   **I wish 가정법, as if 가정법**

22 가정법 과거, 가정법 과거완료

CONCEPT 1 가정법 과거

A 가정법 과거의 형태와 의미

현재 사실에 반대되는 일이나 실현 가능성이 희박한 일을 가정한다.

형태	If+주어+동사의 과거형 ～, 주어+조동사의 과거형+동사원형 ….
의미	만일 ～라면, …일 텐데.
문장 전환	가정법 과거 → 직설법 현재 (긍정 ↔ 부정)

If he were[was] angry, he wouldn't call me.
→ As he isn't angry, he will call me.

If I didn't have my camera, I couldn't take a shot of the tower now.
→ As I have my camera, I can take a shot of the tower now.

B 가정법 과거의 대용 표현

If it were not for the robot, I would do everything alone.
= Were it not for the robot, I would do everything alone.
= Without the robot, I would do everything alone.
= But for the robot, I would do everything alone.

CONCEPT 2 가정법 과거완료

A 가정법 과거완료의 형태와 의미

과거 사실에 반대되는 내용을 가정할 때 사용한다.

형태	If+주어+had+p.p. ～, 주어+조동사의 과거형+have+p.p. ….
의미	만일 ～였다면, …였을 텐데.
문장 전환	가정법 과거완료 → 직설법 과거 (긍정 ↔ 부정)

If he had quit playing the game, he would have gotten a better grade.
→ As he didn't quit playing the game, he didn't get a better grade.

If I hadn't listened to your advice, I couldn't have won the race.
→ As I listened to your advice, I could win the race.

B 가정법 과거완료의 대용 표현

If it had not been for her help, I wouldn't have finished the work.

= Had it not been for her help, I wouldn't have finished the work.

= Without her help, I wouldn't have finished the work.

= But for her help, I wouldn't have finished the work.

GRAMMAR POINT

would와 could

• would는 '의지, 소망'을, could 는 '능력'을 표현할 때 사용한다.

If you were kind to them, they would help you.

(네가 그들에게 친절하다면 그들이 널 도와 줄 텐데.)

If I were a black belt in taekwondo, I could break his nose.

(내가 검은 띠 유단자라면 그의 코를 납작 하게 해줄 수 있을 텐데.)

직설법 조건문과 가정법

• 직설법 조건문

① 불확실한 현재 사실을 가정

② 현재 시제가 미래를 의미

If she has some time, she will visit us.

(그녀가 시간이 있는지 알 수 없음)

• 가정법

① 확실한 현재 사실의 반대를 가 정

② 과거 시제가 현재를 의미

If she had some time, she would visit us.

(그녀는 시간이 없음)

had had

• had+p.p.에서 p.p.가 본동사이 므로 had had 형태도 가능하다.

If she had had enough money, she would have bought the smartphone.

(그녀가 돈이 충분히 있었으면 그 스마트폰 을 샀을 텐데.)

VOCA take a shot of ～의 사진을 찍다 | grade 점수 | quit 그만두다 | advice 충고

Let's Check It Out

>>> 정답 17쪽

A [ ]에서 알맞은 것을 고르시오. 각 1점

1 If I [wore / wear] a raincoat, I wouldn't get wet.

2 If the sky clears up, Sonya [will / would] do the laundry.

3 I [can't / couldn't] have finished the project on time if you had not helped me.

4 Would he [buy / have bought] me *tteokbokki* then if he had had enough money?

5 If you hadn't eaten the last piece of cake, you [wouldn't have had / wouldn't have] a stomachache last night.

6 [Had it not been for / Were it not for] your support, I would have failed.

B 두 문장의 의미가 통하도록 빈칸에 알맞은 말을 쓰시오. 각 1점

1 If she knew the reason, she wouldn't be so angry.

→ As she _____ _____ the reason, she _____ so angry.

2 If I hadn't broken the rule, I wouldn't have paid the fine.

→ As I _____ the rule, I _____ the fine.

3 As Cathy isn't here, she can't look after my son.

→ If Cathy _____ here, she _____ _____ after my son.

4 As we didn't take the highway, we didn't save any time.

→ If we _____ _____ the highway, we _____ _____ _____ some time.

5 If it were not for Photoshop, your legs wouldn't look so long.

→ _____ _____ Photoshop, your legs wouldn't look so long.

6 If it had not been for a face shield, I couldn't have attended the meeting.

→ _____ a face shield, I couldn't have attended the meeting.

VOCA clear up (하늘이) 개다 | stomachache 복통 | fine 벌금 | highway 고속도로 | face shield 얼굴 가리개 | attend a meeting 회의에 참석하다

My score is

Let's Check It Out _____ / 12점

Ready for Exams _____ / 13점

Total _____ / 25점

0~17점 → Level 1 Test

18~21점 → Level 2 Test

22~25점 → Level 3 Test

1 Which correctly translates the given sentence? 2점

> 만약 그녀가 정말로 화가 났다면 나한테 소리를 지를 거야.

① If she were really angry, she will yell at me.

② If she would be really angry, she would yell at me.

③ If she were really angry, she would yell at me.

④ If she is really angry, she would yell at me.

⑤ If she were really angry, she was yell at me.

2 우리말과 같은 뜻이 되도록 빈칸에 알맞은 말로 짝지어진 것은? 3점

> 그녀에게 남자친구가 없었다면 지훈이는 그녀에게 데이트 신청을 했을 것이다.
>
> = If she _____ a boyfriend, Jihun _____ her out.
>
> *ask out: 데이트 신청하다

① had had – would ask

② had had – would have asked

③ didn't have – would ask

④ hadn't had – would ask

⑤ hadn't had – would have asked

3 Choose the <u>necessary</u> words and rearrange them to translate the sentence. Start the sentence with "If." 4점

> 벌이 없다면 무슨 일이 일어날까?
>
> happen, bees, it, happened, what, were, not, for, would, is, if

→ _____, _____?

4 그림을 보고 주어진 단어를 이용해서 빈칸에 알맞은 말을 쓰시오. 4점

→ If he had paid more attention, he _____ _____

_____ his thumb. (hit)

VOCA yell 소리를 지르다 | pay attention 주의를 기울이다 | thumb 엄지

118

UNIT 23 I wish 가정법, as if 가정법

1 I wish 가정법

A I wish 가정법 과거

형태	I wish (that)+주어+동사의 과거형
의미	~라면 좋을 텐데 (현재의 실현 불가능한 소망이나 사실에 대한 유감을 표현)
문장 전환	I wish 가정법 과거 → I am sorry 직설법 현재 (긍정 ↔ 부정)

I wish that I were special. → I am sorry that I am not special.

I wish you had a girlfriend. → I am sorry you don't have a girlfriend.

B I wish 가정법 과거완료

형태	I wish (that)+주어+had+p.p.
의미	~였다면 좋을 텐데 (이루지 못한 과거의 일에 대한 유감을 표현)
문장 전환	I wish 가정법 과거완료 → I am sorry 직설법 과거 (긍정 ↔ 부정)

I wish you had come with me. → I am sorry you didn't come with me.

I wish Jack had driven us home. → I am sorry Jack didn't drive us home.

2 as if 가정법

A as if 가정법 과거

형태	as if[though]+주어+동사의 과거형
의미	마치 ~인 것처럼 (현재 사실과 반대인 상황을 가정)
문장 전환	as if[though] 가정법 과거 → In fact, 직설법 현재 (긍정 ↔ 부정)

She talks as if she were mad at me. → In fact, she isn't mad at me.

He talks as if he knew her. → In fact, he doesn't know her.

B as if 가정법 과거완료

형태	as if[though]+주어+had+p.p.
의미	마치 ~였던 것처럼 (과거 사실과 반대인 상황을 가정)
문장 전환	as if[though] 가정법 과거완료 → In fact, 직설법 과거 (긍정 ↔ 부정)

I felt as if I had had a good nap. → In fact, I hadn't had a good nap.

Yumin behaves as if she hadn't done anything wrong.

→ In fact, Yumin did something wrong.

GRAMMAR POINT

I wished의 시제

- 주절과 종속절이 같은 시제일 때

  I wished I didn't drive a used car.

  → I was sorry I drove a used car.

- 종속절이 주절보다 앞선 시제일 때

  I wished I hadn't bought a used car.

  → I was sorry I had bought a used car.

as if의 시제

- 주절과 종속절이 같은 시제일 때

  She seemed as if she were in a hurry.

  → In fact, she wasn't in a hurry.

- 종속절이 주절보다 앞선 시제일 때

  She seemed as if she had been in a hurry.

  → In fact, she hadn't been in a hurry.

as if 직설법과 가정법의 차이

She looks as if she's rich.

→ Perhaps she is rich.

She talks as if she were rich.

→ In fact, she is not rich.

VOCA special 특별한 | mad 화난 | nap 낮잠 | behave 행동하다

A [ ]에서 알맞은 것을 고르시오. 각 1점

1 I wish that I [am / were] a movie star.

2 I wish I [had had / had] more time then.

3 She looks as if she [saw / had seen] a ghost just now.

4 Mike talked as if he [understood / understands] everything.

5 We acted as though we [didn't play / hadn't played] together the day before.

B 두 문장의 의미가 통하도록 빈칸에 알맞은 말을 쓰시오. 각 1점

1 I wish that I had a sister.

→ I _____ sorry that I _____ _____ a sister.

2 I am sorry you didn't join the military.

→ I _____ you _____ _____ the military.

3 The bear wished it were a human.

→ The bear _____ sorry it _____ a human.

4 Tasha behaves as if she were a princess.

→ _____ _____ , Tasha _____ a princess.

5 In fact, he didn't attend the university.

→ He talks _____ _____ he _____ _____ the university.

C 밑줄 친 부분이 어색하면 고치시오. 각 1점

1 Sometimes I wish I <u>can read</u> your mind.

→ _____

2 I wish that I <u>were born</u> in the 1800s.

→ _____

3 The teacher talks as if the homework <u>was</u> a piece of cake.

→ _____

4 She behaved as if nothing <u>happened</u> the night before.

→ _____

5 I am sorry that he <u>hadn't been</u> able to talk to me last night.

→ _____

VOCA military 군대 | human 인간 | attend 다니다 | piece of cake 식은 죽 먹기(아주 쉬운 일)

120

My score is

Let's Check It Out _____ / 15점   0~17점 → Level 1 Test
Ready for Exams _____ / 10점 → 18~21점 → Level 2 Test
Total _____ / 25점   22~25점 → Level 3 Test

>>> 정답 17쪽

1   Which is suitable for the blank? 2점

> I am sorry my wife can't make it to the party.
> = I wish my wife _____ it to the party.

① makes   ② can make   ③ could make

④ can't make   ⑤ couldn't make

2   다음 문장의 의미를 바르게 이해한 학생은? 2점

> Jinhee talked to me as if she had been hospitalized.

① 미연: 진희는 나에게 진실을 얘기했어.

② 희라: 사실 진희는 병원에 입원하지 않았어.

③ 철우: 진희는 지금도 병원에 있는 게 틀림없어.

④ 누리: 진희는 입원한 것을 유감스럽게 생각해.

⑤ 아미: 글쓴이는 진희가 입원했다고 믿고 있어.

3   우리말과 같은 뜻이 되도록 빈칸에 들어갈 말을 쓰되, 주어진 단어 중에서 <u>필요한 것만</u> 골라 사용하시오. 3점

> 나는 매일 아침 일찍 일어날 수 있었으면 좋겠다. (실제로는 일찍 일어나지 못함)
> want, wish, hope, had, have, get, got, gotten, up, can, could

→ I _____ I _____ _____

_____ early every morning.

4   Look at the picture and complete the translation. 3점

> 여자는 마치 마네킹이 진짜 사람인 것처럼 마네킹과 악수하고 있다.

→ The lady is shaking hands with the dummy _____

_____ it _____ a real man.

VOCA   make it 참석하다 | hospitalize 입원시키다 | shake hands 악수하다 | dummy 마네킹

>>> 정답 17쪽

U22_1A

01 다음 우리말을 영어로 바르게 옮긴 것은? (답 2개) 2점

> 내가 너라면 더 일찍 잠자리에 들 텐데.

① If I am you, I will go to bed earlier.
② If I was you, I would go to bed earlier.
③ If I were you, I will go to bed earlier.
④ If I were you, I would go to bed earlier.
⑤ If I were you, I wouldn't go to bed earlier.

U22_2A

02 Which correction is right? 3점

> Greg didn't come to the party last night.
> If he came, he would have run into his ex-girlfriend.

① didn't come → hasn't come
② If → Whether
③ came → had come
④ would have run → would run
⑤ would have run → wouldn't have run

U23_2A

03 다음 문장을 바르게 이해한 학생은? 2점

> Nick talked as if he had seen a ghost then.

① 권소영: as if 대신 as though나 even if를 써도 돼.
② 김소영: In fact, Nick saw a ghost then.으로 쓸 수 있어.
③ 문소영: 과거 사실과 반대 상황을 가정하므로 had seen을 saw로 써야 해.
④ 박선영: 사실 Nick은 유령을 보지 못했어.
⑤ 이소영: I'm sorry Nick didn't see a ghost.로 바꿔 쓸 수 있어.

U22_2A

04 다음 중 어법상 어색한 것은? 2점

① If he had known your address, he would have sent flowers to you.
② If you had come, the party would have been fun.
③ If I haven't done the work, I would have been fired.
④ If it had not rained, we could have gone to the park.
⑤ If I had had enough time, I would have visited my grandparents.

U23_1B

05 다음 우리말의 의미를 영어로 표현한 두 문장 중 어색한 부분을 찾아 바르게 고친 것은? 4점

★ 고난도

> 어젯밤에 네가 나랑 그 영화를 보지 않아서 유감이야.
>
> ⓐ I wish you hadn't seen the movie with me last night.
> ⓑ I'm sorry you didn't see the movie with me last night.

① ⓐ wish → wished
② ⓐ hadn't seen → had seen
③ ⓐ hadn't seen → saw
④ ⓑ didn't see → saw
⑤ ⓑ didn't see → had seen

U23_1+2+GP

06 문장의 전환이 바르지 못한 것은? (답 2개) 4점

★ 고난도

① I'm sorry I can't speak Japanese well.
  → I wish I could speak Japanese well.
② She swims up the river as if she were a salmon.
  → In fact, she is not a salmon.
③ He talked as if he had heard something.
  → In fact, he hasn't heard anything.
④ I wished I had arrived home on time.
  → I was sorry I didn't arrive home on time.
⑤ I wish that she didn't have a boyfriend.
  → I'm sorry that she has a boyfriend.

U22_1A

07 주어진 표현을 사용해서 우리말을 영작하시오. 4점

> 내게 용기가 있다면, 그에게 말을 걸 텐데.
> have the courage, talk to

→ _____,

_____.

U23_1B

08 주어진 문장과 같은 뜻이 되도록 빈칸에 알맞은 말을 쓰시오. 4점

> I wish you had practiced ballet more often.

→ I am sorry you _____ _____

ballet more often.

U22_2A

09 어법상 어색한 부분을 찾아 바르게 고치시오. 5점

함정

> My parents wouldn't have met if they didn't go to the same university.

_____ → _____

U22_2A

10 우리말과 일치하도록 단어 카드 중에서 빈칸에 알맞은 것을 골라 넣으시오. 7점

★ 고난도

> 내가 중학교 때 모범생이었다면, 컴퓨터 게임을 하지 않았을 텐데.

were	was	not	been	had	have
won't	wouldn't	play	played		

→ If I _____ _____ a model

student during middle school, I

_____ _____ _____

computer games.

U22_1B

11 Rearrange the words to fill in the blank. 4점

> it, for, were, not, water

→ _____, no

living things could exist.

U23_1B

12 다음 두 문장의 의미가 같도록 빈칸을 채우시오. 4점

> I wish Mr. Jackson had had enough time then.

→ I'm sorry _____

_____.

U23_1A

13 조건에 맞도록 빈칸 (A)에 알맞은 말을 써서 남편의 말을 완성하시오. 5점

함정

Husband:	Honey, ___(A)___ every day.
Wife:	Why don't you cook yourself then?

· 조건 1 I wish 구문을 사용할 것
· 조건 2 동사의 시제에 유의할 것
· 조건 3 어휘 – not have the same meal
· 조건 4 빈칸에 8단어로 쓸 것

(A) _____

U23_2B+GP

14 Find the sentence that has an error and correct it. 5점

한눈에 쏙

> ⓐ They look as if they fought just now.
> ⓑ I wished I didn't have a sister like you.

(___) _____ → _____

U23_GP

15 다음 상황을 읽고 문장을 완성하시오. 5점

> Kyle and I went to the same school. We bumped into each other on the street yesterday. I was so happy to see my old friend that I shouted, "Hey, Kyle! Is that you?" However, he pretended he was looking somewhere else.
>
> *bump into: ~와 우연히 만나다

→ Kyle acted _____ me.

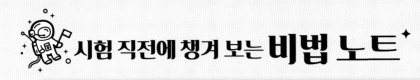

한눈에 쏙! 아래 노트를 보면서 빈칸을 채워 보세요.

1 **가정법 과거** → 1)_____ 사실의 반대

• If+주어+과거 동사 ~, 주어+조동사 과거형+동사원형

예문) If he were angry, he wouldn't call me.

2 **가정법 과거완료** → 2)_____ 사실의 반대

• If+주어+had+p.p. ~, 주어+조동사 과거형+have+p.p.

예문) If he had been angry, he wouldn't have called me.

3 **I wish 가정법**

• I wish+과거 (뜻: 1)_____) → 2)_____+현재

• I wish+had+p.p. (뜻: 3)_____) → 4)_____+과거
  과거완료

4 **as if 가정법**

• as if+과거 (뜻: 1)_____) → In fact, 현재

• as if+had+p.p. (뜻: 2)_____) → In fact, 과거

헷갈리지 말자! 초록색으로 표시된 부분을 바르게 고쳐 쓰세요.

1 If I knew her number, I will call her.

2 If he had worn a mask, he wouldn't had gotten the disease.

3 We spoke to the teacher as if we didn't go to the Internet cafe.

CHAPTER 12
특수 구문

UNIT 24   **강조, 생략**
UNIT 25   **도치**

CONCEPT 1 강조 구문

동사 강조	do/does/did+동사원형	He did meet the actress yesterday.
명사 강조	the very+명사	She's the very girl I've been looking for.
It ~ that 강조	It is/was+강조어+that ~	It was Mary that got a perfect score.

A It ~ that... 강조 구문에서 사용되는 관계사

It ~ that... 강조 구문(…하는 것은 바로 ~이다)에서 강조하는 대상에 따라 that 대신에 who, when, where 등을 사용할 수 있다.

Mary got a perfect score on the last exam.
　　① 　② 　　③ 　　　　④

① It was Mary that[who] got a perfect score on the last exam. (주어 강조)

② Mary did get a perfect score on the last exam. (동사 강조)

③ It was a perfect score that Mary got on the last exam. (목적어 강조)

④ It was on the last exam that[when] Mary got a perfect score.
　　(시간 부사구 강조)

B It ~ that... 강조 구문 vs. It ~ that... 가주어-진주어 구문

It ~ that... 강조 구문	It ~ that... 가주어-진주어 구문
It is/was+명사/부사구 등+that …	It is/was+형용사+that …
강조어구를 that 이하로 보낼 때 자연스러운 문장이 됨	It ~ that 사이에 위치한 어구를 that 이하로 보낼 때 문장 성립이 안 됨
It was Mary that[who] got a perfect score. = Mary got a perfect score. (Mary가 that절의 주어)	It is true that stress affects health. ≠ Stress affects health true. (true가 that 이하의 문장에 포함되지 않음)

가주어-진주어 구문

• 주어의 길이가 길 경우 주어 자리에 가주어 it을 쓰고 진주어는 문장 뒤로 보낸 구문을 말한다.

That most people want security rather than liberty is true.

→ It is true that most people want security rather than liberty.

(대부분의 사람들이 자유보다 안전을 더 원한다는 것은 사실이다.)

CONCEPT 2 생략

반복되는 어구	Some stars appear red, and others (appear) blue.
목적격 관계대명사	This is the book (which[that]) I bought yesterday.
주격 관계대명사+be동사	I read a novel (which[that] was) written in English.
부사절에서 주어+be동사	While (I was) walking on the street, I heard this song.
to부정사(대부정사)	I can't save as much money as I want to (save).
재귀대명사(강조 용법)	He repaired the bike (himself).

'주어 + be동사' 생략

• when, while, as, if, though 등의 접속사가 이끄는 부사절에서 주어가 주절의 주어와 반드시 일치해야 생략이 가능하다.

When (he was) asked a personal question, he felt a little offended.

(개인적인 질문을 받았을 때 그는 약간 불쾌하게 느꼈다.)

VOCA affect 영향을 미치다 | security 안전 | liberty 자유 | personal 개인적인 | offend 기분 상하게 하다

Let's Check It Out

>>> 정답 18쪽

A 빈칸에 강조하는 말을 넣어서 문장을 완성하시오. 각 1점

1 A: Is there a job for me here?

   B: Yes, we _____ have a perfect job for you.

2 A: She is the _____ woman that I told you about.

   B: Do you mean the one you see on the bus every morning?

3 A: Did you really send the AirPods? I haven't gotten them yet.

   B: Sure. I _____ _____ them. Trust me.

B 밑줄 친 부분을 강조하는 문장을 완성하시오. 각 1점

1 <u>Benny</u> bought a new phone.

   → It _____ _____ that bought a new phone.

2 Benny bought <u>a new phone</u>.

   → _____ _____ _____ _____ _____ that
   Benny bought.

3 I happened to see Chris on the street <u>yesterday</u>.

   → It was _____ that I _____ _____ _____
   _____ on the street.

C 다음 문장이 '강조 구문'인지 '가주어-진주어 구문'인지 구분하시오. 각 1점

1 It was at the library that I first met her.   → _____

2 It is fortunate that you speak English fluently. → _____

3 It is strange that we've never met before.   → _____

4 It is not every flower that smells sweet.   → _____

D 생략할 수 있는 부분에 <u>모두</u> 괄호로 표시하시오. 각 1점

1 A: Would you like to go to the movies tonight?

   B: I'd love to go, but I can't.

2 Though I was tired, I decided to do what I had to do.

3 You need to throw away all the things that you don't need.

4 You should have called the police when I told you to call the police.

5 Line dancing was started by women who were waiting to use the bathroom.

VOCA happen to 우연히 ~하다 | fortunate 운이 좋은 | fluently 유창하게

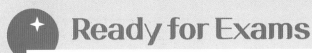

My score is

Let's Check It Out _____ / 15점   0~17점 → Level 1 Test
Ready for Exams _____ / 10점 ⟹ 18~21점 → Level 2 Test
Total _____ / 25점   22~25점 → Level 3 Test

Ready for Exams

>>> 정답 18쪽

---

1   다음 중 밑줄 친 부분의 쓰임이 다른 하나는? 2점

① It was Jessica that got married to Josh.

② It was not true that he could not afford it.

③ It was in the hospital that I saw Bruce.

④ It was my niece that pushed my wheelchair.

⑤ It was in 2018 that I graduated from high school.

---

2   Who finds the error and corrects it properly? (2 answers) 3점

> ⓐ It was yesterday that he finished reading the book.
> ⓑ He did went to the magic school.
> ⓒ It was I what made a mistake.

① 영제: ⓐ that → when   ② 장현: ⓐ that → what

③ 윤성: ⓑ did → does   ④ 진유: ⓑ went → go

⑤ 영준: ⓒ what → who

---

3   Write the proper sentence for blank (A) according to the conditions. 5점

A: I went to the library yesterday, and I saw Judy studying there.
B: Who?
A: _____ (A) _____
B: Really? I can't believe it. She's the last person I would expect to see in the library.

· Condition 1   강조 구문을 사용할 것
· Condition 2   과거 시제로 쓸 것
· Condition 3   9단어로 쓸 것

(A) _____

VOCA   afford ~을 살 능력이 되다 | expect 기대하다

128

도치

CONCEPT
1 ## 강조를 위한 도치

GRAMMAR POINT

장소 부사(구)가 문장 첫머리에 올 때	주어가 명사인 경우: 부사(구)+동사+주어
	There goes my career! (내 앞길은 끝장이군!)
	주어가 대명사인 경우: 부사(구)+주어+동사
	There he stood like a statue. (그는 동상처럼 거기 서 있었다.)
부정어(구)가 문장 첫머리에 올 때	be동사가 쓰인 경우: 부정어(구)+be동사+주어
	He is seldom passionate about school. → Seldom is he passionate about school. (그는 공부에 거의 열정이 없다.)
	일반동사/조동사가 쓰인 경우: 부정어(구)+조동사+주어+본동사
	She hardly answered directly. → Hardly did she answer directly. (그녀는 거의 바로 대답하지 않았다.) I have never deceived anybody. → Never have I deceived anybody. (나는 누구도 속인 적이 없다.)

도치를 할 수 없는 경우

- 장소인 경우 타동사가 나오면 도치를 할 수 없다.

  I lost my passport at the airport.
  → At the airport lost I my passport. (×)
  → At the airport, I lost my passport. (○)

주어가 대명사일 때

- There로 시작하는 문장에서 주어가 대명사이면 도치되지 않는다.

  There he goes. (○)
  There goes he. (×)

A 유도부사로 쓰인 there는 어법상 주어의 역할을 하며 주어와 동사가 도치된다.

There the teacher goes. (×) → There goes the teacher. (○)

B 부정어구(not, no, never, hardly, seldom 등)에 의한 도치가 일어날 때 시제에 따른 조동사와 본동사의 형태에 주의해야 한다.

① 현재/과거: 부정어구+조동사(do/does/did/can...)+주어+동사원형

He could hardly contain himself.

→ Hardly could he contain himself.

② 완료: 부정어구+조동사(had/have/has)+주어+과거분사

Connie has never complained about it.

→ Never has Connie complained about it.

CONCEPT
2 ## 어법상 도치

so/neither 가 문장 첫머 리에 올 경우	So+조동사/be동사+주어
	A: I like the design of the suit. (나는 그 정장의 디자인이 좋아.) B: So do I. = I like the design, too. (나도 그래. – 긍정에 대한 동의)
	Neither+조동사/be동사+주어
	A: I am not qualified to teach them. (나는 그들을 가르칠 만한 자격이 안 돼.) B: Neither am I. = I am not qualified either. (나도 안 돼. – 부정에 대한 동의)
가정법에서 if의 생략	(If)+동사+주어 ~, 주어+동사
	If I were you, I wouldn't do that. → Were I you, I wouldn't do that.

VOCA   career 직업, 진로 | statue 동상, 조각상 | passionate 열정적인 | deceive 속이다 | contain oneself 자제하다 | qualified 자격이 있는

Let's Check It Out

>>> 정답 18쪽

A 밑줄 친 부분을 강조하는 문장을 완성하시오. 각 1점

1 Some coins were in my pocket.

→ In my pocket _____ _____ _____ .

2 I have never seen such wonderful scenery.

→ Never _____ _____ _____ such wonderful scenery.

3 She could hardly control her temper.

→ Hardly _____ _____ _____ her temper.

B 괄호 안의 지시대로 문장을 다시 쓸 때, 빈칸에 알맞은 말을 쓰시오. 각 1점

1 If she were in my shoes, she would do the same thing. (If 생략)

→ _____ , she would do the same thing.

2 The second bathroom is beside her bedroom. (밑줄 친 부분을 강조)

→ Beside her bedroom _____ .

3 He was so ambitious that he could reach his goal. (밑줄 친 부분을 강조)

→ So ambitious _____ he could reach his goal.

4 He is not only an actor but also a director. (밑줄 친 부분을 강조)

→ Not only _____ , but he is also a director.

5 The fountain stands in the middle of the city. (밑줄 친 부분을 강조)

→ In the middle of the city _____ .

C 밑줄 친 B의 응답과 같은 뜻의 문장을 쓰시오. 각 1점

1 A: I am so confused now.

B: I'm so confused, too.

→ _____ _____ _____ .

2 A: She can't afford to rent her own apartment.

B: I can't either.

→ _____ _____ _____ .

3 A: I don't agree with James.

B: Me neither.

→ _____ _____ _____ .

VOCA scenery 경치, 풍경 | control 통제하다 | temper 기질, 성질 | ambitious 야심 있는 | director 감독 | fountain 분수

1 밑줄 친 부분을 강조한 문장으로 알맞은 것은? 2점

> We should <u>never</u> exclude the possibility of peaceful unification.

① Should we never exclude the possibility of peaceful unification.

② It was never that we should exclude the possibility of peaceful unification.

③ It was never that should we exclude the possibility of peaceful unification.

④ Never should we exclude the possibility of peaceful unification.

⑤ Never we should exclude the possibility of peaceful unification.

2 밑줄 친 문장을 간단히 줄여 쓸 때 빈칸에 알맞은 것은? 2점

> Birds, rain, and wind make a kind of music.
> The sea makes a kind of music, too. (= _____ the sea.)

① So do   ② So did   ③ So does

④ So have   ⑤ So is

3 Rewrite the sentence correctly according to the conditions. 각 3점

> Near the river, a small village lies.
> ·Condition 두 개의 문장을 쓰되 (1)은 도치문으로 쓸 것

(1) _____

(2) _____

4 조건에 맞도록 주어진 문장을 다시 쓰시오. 4점

> Though invited to the event, she couldn't attend it.
> ·조건 1 생략된 부분을 포함해서 문장을 다시 쓰시오.
> ·조건 2 모두 11단어로 쓸 것

➡ _____

VOCA exclude 배제하다 | possibility 가능성 | peaceful 평화적인 | unification 통일 | village 마을 | attend 참석하다

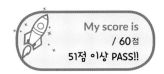
>>> 정답 19쪽

U24_1

01 밑줄 친 부분을 강조할 때 빈칸에 알맞은 것은? 2점

> __Necessity__ makes people invent things.
> → _____ necessity _____ makes people invent things.

① It is – that
② It was – that
③ It so – that
④ It does – that
⑤ It be – that

U24_1

02 밑줄 친 부분의 쓰임이 [보기]와 <u>다른</u> 하나는? 2점

> I __do__ have trouble hearing you because of that loud music.

① You __did__ have a good handle on that.
② I __do__ like things being created by teams.
③ He __did__ go there by himself.
④ I'll __do__ my homework after dinner.
⑤ They __do__ love their teacher.

U24_1

03 다음 중 어법상 올바른 문장은 <u>모두</u> 몇 개인가? 4점

★ 고난도

> ⓐ It was her ID card that I found on the bus.
> ⓑ It was on the bus that I found her ID card.
> ⓒ It was I that found her ID card on the bus.
> ⓓ I did found her ID card on the bus.
> ⓔ It was on the bus which I found her ID card.

① 1개
② 2개
③ 3개
④ 4개
⑤ 5개

U24_1+GP

04 Which answer choice has a <u>different</u> usage for the underlined words? 3점

✔ 함정

① __It was__ at the bus stop __that__ they first met.
② __It was__ important __that__ we learned how to drive.
③ __Was it__ her advice __that__ made you give up?
④ __It was__ last year __when__ I went to Europe.
⑤ __It was__ Jenny __who__ made a mistake.

U24_2+GP

05 Which of the underlined words CANNOT be omitted? 2점

① I don't wear makeup because I don't want to __wear makeup__.
② Such a fertilizer would cause less pollution when __it is__ washed away.
③ She cooked this pasta __herself__.
④ I had a pen __which was__ made of silver.
⑤ To some, life is joy; to others, life is __pain__.

U25_2

06 다음 문장의 빈칸에 알맞은 것은? 2점

> Mary likes dancing, and so _____ Mike.
> Mary는 춤추는 것을 좋아한다. Mike도 그렇다.

① do
② does
③ did
④ is
⑤ am

U25_1

07 다음에 대해 바르게 설명한 학생을 <u>모두</u> 고르시오. 3점

 한눈에 쏙

> ⓐ There goes an ambulance.
> ⓑ There goes he.

① 선주: ⓐ는 There가 문장 앞으로 가서 주어와 동사가 도치된 문장으로 틀린 것이 없다.
② 장현: There가 문장 앞에 있어도 보통명사가 주어일 때는 도치하지 않으므로 ⓐ는 틀린 문장이다.
③ 종윤: ⓑ는 도치된 올바른 문장이다.
④ 희석: ⓑ에서 goes he는 he goes여야 한다.
⑤ 민서: ⓑ에서 goes he는 does he go여야 한다.

U25_1

08 Choose ALL of the correct translations. 3점

 한눈에 쏙

> 저는 밤에는 거의 커피를 마시지 않아요.

① Seldom have I coffee at night.
② Seldom do I have coffee at night.
③ Seldom I have coffee at night.
④ I have seldom coffee at night.
⑤ I seldom have coffee at night.

09 U24_1
주어진 문장을 우리말과 같은 의미의 강조 구문으로 다시 쓸 때 빈칸에 알맞은 말을 쓰시오. 4점

> I met Jessie in the park yesterday.
> → 내가 Jessie를 공원에서 만난 것은 바로 어제였다.

→ It was _____ _____ I met Jessie in the park.

10 U24_2
★ 고난도
두 문장이 같은 뜻이 되도록 빈칸에 알맞은 말을 쓰시오. 6점

> Paris is an exciting city. It is the largest city in France.

→ Paris, _____ _____ the largest city in France, is an exciting city.

11 U24_1
빈칸에 강조하는 말을 넣어 문장을 완성하시오. 4점

> The thought of meeting him makes me nervous.

→ The _____ thought of meeting him makes me nervous.

12 U24_2
다음 문장에서 생략된 부분을 넣어 문장을 다시 쓰시오.
5점

> If used properly, robots can be very useful.

→ _____
_____

13 U25_2
밑줄 친 B의 응답과 같은 뜻이 되도록 빈칸에 알맞은 말을 쓰시오. 5점

> A: It was a wonderful party. I enjoyed it a lot.
> B: I enjoyed it, too.

→ _____ _____ _____ _____ .

14 U25_2
Translate the underlined Korean sentence into English according to the conditions. 각 4점

> A: Never have I heard such a strange story.
> B: 나도 그래.
>
> ·Condition 1   두 문장으로 답할 것
> ·Condition 2   각각 3단어로 쓸 것

(1) _____
(2) _____

15 U24_2
★ 고난도
다음 대화에서 밑줄 친 (A)를 영어로 옮기시오. 7점

> Q: If you were given a chance to date a celebrity, who would you choose?
> A: (A) 내가 유명인과 데이트할 기회를 얻는다면, I would choose the movie star Kim Suhyun.
> *celebrity: 유명인
>
> ·조건   가정법을 쓰되 if를 쓰지 말 것

(A) _____

시험 직전에 챙겨 보는 비법 노트

한눈에 쏙! 아래 노트를 보면서 빈칸을 채워 보세요.

1 강조 구문

① 동사 강조	1)_____ / 2)_____ / 3)_____ +동사원형
② 명사 강조	the 4)_____ +명사
③ It ~ that... 강조	It is/was 5)_____ / 6)_____ / 7)_____ that... → It is/was ~ that 생략해도 8)_____ 구조*

*cf. It ~ that 가주어-진주어 구문: It is/was ~ that 생략하면 9)_____ 구조

2 생략

- 반복어구
- 관계대명사 1)_____ 또는 2)_____ +3)_____
- 부사절에서 4)_____ *+5)_____   *주절의 주어와 같을 때
- 6)대_____
- 재귀대명사의 7)_____ 용법

3 도치

- 장소 부사구+1)_____ +2)_____ *   *주어가 대명사이면 도치 안 함
- 부정어구+3)_____ / 4)_____ +5)_____
- 가정법 과거 도치: 6)_____ +7)_____ ~

헷갈리지 말자! 초록색으로 표시된 부분을 바르게 고쳐 쓰세요.

1 We couldn't read the menu writing in Spanish.

2 While walked on ice, he slipped and fell.

3 Never he has trusted anyone in his life.

불규칙 동사 변화표

불규칙 동사도
외우는 방법이 있다!

1 A – A – A 형태 동일

원형	뜻	과거	과거분사
broadcast	방송하다	broadcast	broadcast
bet	돈을 걸다	bet	bet
burst	파열하다	burst	burst
cast	던지다	cast	cast
cost	비용이 들다	cost	cost
★cut	자르다	cut	cut
forecast	예고하다	forecast	forecast
★hit	치다	hit	hit
hurt	아프게 하다	hurt	hurt
let	~하게 하다	let	let
★put	놓다	put	put
quit	~을 그만두다	quit	quit
★read	읽다	read [red]	read [red]
rid	~을 제거하다	rid	rid
set	놓다	set	set
shed	흘리다	shed	shed
shut	닫다	shut	shut
spit	침을 뱉다	spit	spit
split	쪼개다	split	split
spread	펴다	spread	spread
thrust	찌르다	thrust	thrust
upset	뒤엎다	upset	upset

2 A – A – A' 과거분사만 살짝 바뀜

원형	뜻	과거	과거분사
beat	때리다, 이기다	beat	beaten

3 A – B – A 과거형에서 모음만 바뀜

원형	뜻	과거	과거분사
★come	오다	came	come
★become	되다	became	become
★run	달리다	ran	run

4 A – B – A'   과거형은 모음 변화, 과거분사형은 원형에 –n 붙임

원형	뜻	과거	과거분사
arise [əráiz]	(일이) 일어나다	arose [əróuz]	arisen [ərizn]
*be (am, is, are)	~이다	was, were	been
blow	불다	blew [blu:]	blown [bloun]
*do, does	하다	did	done
draw	당기다, 그리다	drew [dru:]	drawn [drɔ:n]
*drive	운전하다	drove [drouv]	driven [drivn]
*eat	먹다	ate	eaten
fall	떨어지다	fell	fallen
forbid	금지하다	forbade	forbidden
forgive	용서하다	forgave	forgiven
forsake	그만두다, 저버리다	forsook	forsaken
*give	주다	gave [ɡeiv]	given [ɡivn]
*go	가다	went [went]	gone [ɡɔ:n]
*grow	자라다	grew [ɡru:]	grown [ɡroun]
*know	알다	knew [nju:]	known [noun]
ride	(차, 말 등을) 타다	rode [roud]	ridden [ridn]
rise	일어서다	rose [rouz]	risen [rizn]
*see	보다	saw [sɔ:]	seen [si:n]
shake	흔들다	shook [ʃuk]	shaken [ʃeikn]
show	보여주다, 보이다	showed	shown, showed
sow [sou]	(씨를) 뿌리다	sowed [soud]	sown [soun]
strive	노력하다	strove [strouv]	striven [strivn]
*take	잡다	took [tuk]	taken [teikn]
thrive	번영하다	throve [θrouv], thrived	thriven [θrivn], thrived
*throw	던지다	threw [θru:]	thrown [θroun]
withdraw	물러나다	withdrew [wiðdrú:]	withdrawn [wiðdrɔ́:n]
*write	쓰다	wrote [rout]	written [ritn]

5 A – B – B   원형에 –t 붙임

원형	뜻	과거	과거분사
bend	구부리다	bent	bent
*build	세우다	built	built
burn	태우다	burnt, burned	burnt, burned
deal	다루다	dealt [delt]	dealt
dwell	거주하다, 살다	dwelt, dwelled	dwelt, dwelled
lend	빌려주다	lent	lent
mean	의미하다	meant [ment]	meant
*send	보내다	sent	sent
smell	냄새 맡다, 냄새가 나다	smelt, smelled	smelt, smelled

| spend | 소비하다 | spent | spent |
| spoil | 망쳐놓다 | spoilt, spoiled | spoilt, spoiled |

6 A – B – B 원형의 자음 + ought/aught

원형	뜻	과거	과거분사
*bring	가져오다	brought [brɔːt]	brought
*buy	사다	bought [bɔːt]	bought
*catch	잡다	caught [kɔːt]	caught
*fight	싸우다	fought [fɔːt]	fought
seek	찾다	sought [sɔːt]	sought
*teach	가르치다	taught [tɔːt]	taught
*think	생각하다	thought [θɔːt]	thought

7 A – B – B 원형의 자음 + ound

원형	뜻	과거	과거분사
bind	묶다	bound [baund]	bound
*find	발견하다	found [faund]	found

8 A – B – B 원형의 모음이 하나로 줄고 + t

원형	뜻	과거	과거분사
creep	기다, 포복하다	crept [krept]	crept
*feel	느끼다	felt	felt
*keep	유지하다	kept	kept
kneel [niːl]	무릎 꿇다, 굴복하다	knelt [nelt]	knelt
*leave	떠나다	left	left
*lose [luːz]	잃다	lost [lɔːst]	lost
*sleep	자다	slept	slept
sweep	쓸다	swept [swept]	swept

9 A – B – B 원형의 모음이 하나로 줄어듦

원형	뜻	과거	과거분사
feed	먹이다	fed [fed]	fed
*meet	만나다	met [met]	met
shoot [ʃuːt]	쏘다	shot [ʃɑt]	shot

10 A – B – B y를 i로 바꾸고 -d를 붙임

원형	뜻	과거	과거분사
lay	두다	laid [leid]	laid
*pay	지불하다	paid [peid]	paid
*say	말하다	said [sed]	said

11 A – B – B 원형에서 모음만 바뀜

원형	뜻	과거	과거분사
behold	～를 보다	beheld	beheld
bleed	피를 흘리다	bled	bled
breed	기르다	bred	bred
cling	달라붙다	clung	clung
dig	파다	dug [dʌg]	dug
fling	내던지다	flung	flung
hang	걸다	hung	hung
*hold	잡다, 손에 들다	held	held
lead	이끌다	led	led
shine	빛나다	shone [ʃoun]	shone
*sit	앉다	sat [sæt]	sat
spin	(실을) 잣다	spun [spʌn]	spun
*stand	서다	stood [stud]	stood
stick	찌르다	stuck	stuck
sting	쏘다	stung	stung
strike	때리다	struck [strʌk]	struck
*win	이기다	won [wʌn]	won
wind [waind]	감다	wound [waund]	wound
withhold	보류하다	withheld	withheld

12 A – B – B 모음 변화, 끝에 -d 붙임

원형	뜻	과거	과거분사
flee	도망치다	fled [fled]	fled
*have, has	가지다	had	had
*hear [hiər]	듣다	heard [həːrd]	heard
*make	만들다	made	made
*sell	팔다	sold	sold
slide	미끄러지다	slid	slid
*tell	말하다	told	told

13 A – B – B' 모음 변화, 과거형 + n

원형	뜻	과거	과거분사
awake [əwéik]	깨다	awoke [əwóuk]	awoken [əwoukn]
*bear [bɛər]	낳다	bore [bɔər]	born [bɔːrn]
bite	물다	bit [bit]	bitten [bitn]
*break	깨뜨리다	broke [brouk]	broken [broukn]
*choose	고르다	chose [tʃouz]	chosen [tʃouzn]
*forget	잊다	forgot [fərgát]	forgotten [fərgátn]
freeze	얼음이 얼다	froze [frouz]	frozen [frouzn]
*get	얻다	got [gɑt]	gotten [gɑtn]
*hide	감추다	hid [hid]	hidden [hidn]
*speak	말하다	spoke [spouk]	spoken [spoukn]
steal	훔치다	stole [stoul]	stolen [stouln]
swear	맹세하다	swore [swɔər]	sworn [swɔːrn]
tear [tɛər]	찢다	tore [tɔər]	torn [tɔːrn]
tread [tred]	걷다, 짓밟다	trod [trɑd]	trodden [trɑdn]
wake	깨다	woke	woken
*wear	입다	wore [wɔər]	worn [wɔːrn]

14 A – B – C

원형	뜻	과거	과거분사
*begin	시작하다	began [bigǽn]	begun [bigʌ́n]
*drink	마시다	drank [dræŋk]	drunk [drʌŋk]
*fly	날다	flew [fluː]	flown [floun]
lie	가로눕다	lay [lei]	lain [lein]
cf. lie (규칙 변화)	거짓말하다	lied	lied
*ring	울리다	rang [ræŋ]	rung [rʌŋ]
shrink	줄어들다	shrank [ʃræŋk]	shrunk [ʃrʌŋk]
*sing	노래하다	sang [sæŋ]	sung [sʌŋ]
sink	가라앉나	sank [sæŋk]	sunk [sʌŋk]
spring	튀다	sprang [spræŋ]	sprung [sprʌŋ]
*swim	수영하다	swam [swæm]	swum [swʌm]

15 조동사

원형	뜻	과거
*must	~해야 한다	(had to)
*can	~할 수 있다	could [cud]
*may	~해도 좋다	might [mait]
shall	~할 것이다	should [ʃud]
*will	~할 것이다	would [wud]

16 뜻에 따라 활용이 달라지는 불규칙 동사

원형	뜻	과거	과거분사
bear	참다	bore	borne
	낳다	bore	born
bid	명령하다	bade	bidden
	말하다	bid	bid
hang	걸다	hung	hung
	교수형에 처하다	hanged	hanged

17 혼동하기 쉬운 불규칙 동사와 규칙 동사

원형	뜻	과거	과거분사
bind	묶다	bound [baund]	bound
bound [baund]	되튀다	bounded	bounded
fall	떨어지다, 쓰러지다	fell	fallen
fell	쓰러뜨리다	felled	felled
find	발견하다	found [faund]	found
found [faund]	세우다, 창립하다	founded	founded
fly	날다	flew [flu:]	flown [floun]
flow	흐르다	flowed	flowed
lie	눕다	lay	lain
lay	눕히다, 낳다	laid	laid
see	보다	saw	seen
saw [sɔː]	톱질하다	sawed [sɔːd]	sawed, sawn [sɔːn]
sew [sou]	바느질하다	sewed [soud]	sewed, sewn [soun]
sit	앉다	sat	sat
set	두다	set	set
wind	감다	wound [waund]	wound
wound [wuːnd]	상처를 입히다	wounded	wounded
welcome	환영하다	welcomed	welcomed
overcome	이겨내다, 극복하다	overcame	overcome

MEMO

MEMO

MEMO

신영주

2급 외국어 정교사 자격증, UCSD TESOL취득(국제영어교사 교육자격증, University of California)
(전) EBSi 온라인 강사, 대치 시대인재, 이강학원 강사
(현) 프라우드 세븐 어학원 원장, 리딩타운 원장
저서: 체크체크, 올백(천재교육), 투탑 영어(디딤돌), Grammar 콕, VOCA콕(꿈을담는틀), 중학 영문법 클리어(동아) 등 다수의 교재 공저

이건희

쥬기스(http://jugis.co.kr) 대표
저서: 맨처음 수능 시리즈 – 맨처음 수능 영문법, 맨처음 수능 영어(기본, 실력, 독해, 완성)
　　　내공 시리즈 – 내공 중학영문법, 내공 중학 영어구문, 내공 중학영어듣기 모의고사 20회
　　　체크체크(천재교육), Grammar In(비상교육) 외 다수
instagram@gunee27

최신개정판

내신공략 중학영문법 **3** 개념이해책

지은이 신영주, 이건희
펴낸이 정규도
펴낸곳 (주)다락원

개정판 1쇄 발행 2021년 3월 15일
개정판 6쇄 발행 2024년 3월 15일

편집 김민주, 서정아
디자인 구수정
조판 블랙엔화이트
영문 감수 Michael A. Putlack
삽화 김진용

다락원 경기도 파주시 문발로 211
내용문의: (02)736-2031 내선 532
구입문의: (02)736-2031 내선 250~252
Fax: (02)732-2037
출판등록 1977년 9월 16일 제406-2008-000007호

ISBN 978-89-277-0893-3 54740
　　　978-89-277-0888-9 54740(set)

http://www.darakwon.co.kr
다락원 홈페이지를 방문하시면 상세한 출판 정보와 함께 동영상 강좌,
MP3 자료 등 다양한 어학 정보를 얻으실 수 있습니다.

내공 신공략 중학영문법

신영주 ✦ 이건희 지음

최신개정판

신유형과 고난도 서술형 문제로 중학영어 내신 완벽 대비

개념이해책

3

정답 및 해설

DARAKWON

내_신공_략
중학영문법

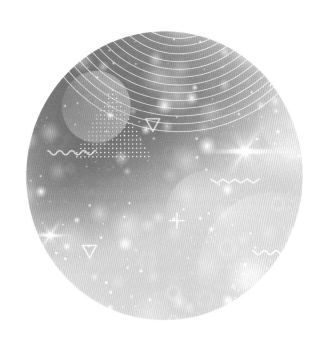

개념이해책 3
정답 및 해설

CHAPTER 01
문장의 구조

 01 주어, 목적어, 주격 보어

Let's Check It Out

p. 13

A 1 Planning 2 The young
3 When to start
4 Whether he will come
5 what I think 6 What I dream

B 1 helping 2 to eat
3 that 4 seeing
5 soft 6 have
7 healthy

C 1 The man whom we met
2 What you picked up
3 that she didn't tell a lie
4 much more confident
5 what to select

Ready for Exams

p. 14

1 ① 2 ③
3 surrounded by small people
4 It is certain that he will win the game.

해설

1 ① 문장의 주어가 되기 위해 명사절로 만들 접속사 that이 필요하다. (→ That you do your best)

2 ⓐ 완전한 문장을 목적절로 만들어 줄 접속사 that이 알맞다. (what → that) ⓒ 주격 보어로 부사가 아닌 형용사가 와야 한다. (silently → silent)

3 주격 보어로 '둘러싸인'이라는 의미의 과거분사 surrounded가 알맞다.

4 he will win the game이라는 문장을 주어로 만들기 위해 앞에 접속사 that을 쓰고, 단어 수를 맞추기 위해 that절을 문장 뒤로 보내고 가주어 It을 쓴다.

02 목적격 보어

Let's Check It Out

p. 16

A 1 the *Queen Mary* 2 her
3 to be 4 cry
5 carried 6 singing

B 1 sad 2 run 또는 running
3 to talk 4 called

5 love 또는 to love

C 1 made us get up at 6 o'clock
2 asked her to come to the party
3 help me write my essay
4 the cup broken
5 told us to be on time for online classes

Ready for Exams

p. 17

1 ① 2 ③
3 Exercise can help you stay healthy.
4 The general ordered the soldier to run.

해설

1 make(사역동사)+목적어+동사원형

2 ·see(지각동사)+목적어+동사원형/현재분사
·help(준사역동사)+목적어+동사원형/to부정사
·let(사역동사)+목적어+동사원형

3 「help+목적어+동사원형」 구문이다. stay는 2형식 동사로 뒤에 형용사가 온다. (운동은 당신이 건강한 상태를 유지하도록 도울 수 있다.)

4 order동사는 목적격 보어로 to부정사를 취한다.

Review Test

p. 18

01 ① ⑤ 02 ① ③
03 ② ④ ⑤ 04 ①
05 ⑤ 06 ②
07 ② 08 ②
09 Truth doesn't ever change.
10 What we know is not everything.
11 staying → to stay
12 remained friends
13 The desk in the classroom is made of glass.
14 asked me to help him with his homework
15 When did you have your house remodeled?
16 her crying in her room

해설

01 It ~ to... 가주어-진주어 구문으로 바꾸거나 to부정사 대신에 동명사를 써도 주어 역할을 할 수 있다.

02 The poor were helped by the ordinary. 또는 Poor people were helped by ordinary people.로 영작할 수 있다. 'the+형용사'는 복수 취급하므로 복수 동사 were가 알맞다.

03 The kid는 단수 주어이므로 주격 관계대명사 who(생략 불가)가 이끄는 절이 끝나는 son까지가 주어부로 동사는 has가 알맞다. 주어 The kid(그 아이)가 musical talent(음악적 재능)를 가지고 있는 것이 맞다.

04 we do 앞에 불완전한 문장을 이끌어 줄 관계사 what이 필요하다. (→ What we do is more valuable than what we think.)

05 make동사는 목적격 보어로 동사원형이 온다. (Suji to dance → Suji dance)

06 지각동사 see는 목적격 보어로 동사원형이나 -ing가 올 수

2

있다. to enjoy 대신 enjoy[enjoying]가 되어야 한다.

07 help는 목적격 보어로 동사원형과 to부정사만 올 수 있다.
(climbing → climb 또는 to climb)

08 ⓐ sit → to sit ⓓ to keep → keep[keeping]

09 true는 형용사이므로 주어가 되기 위해서는 명사형 truth로
써야 한다.

10 불완전한 문장 we know를 주어로 만들 관계사 what이 필
요하다.

11 want동사는 to부정사를 목적어로 취한다.

12 2형식 동사 remain의 보어로 명사 friends가 사용된 문장
이다.

13 전치사구가 포함된 명사구가 주어로 쓰였다.
(be made of: ～로 만들어지다)

14 ask동사는 목적격 보어로 to부정사를 취한다.

15 집이 리모델링을 받는 수동의 관계이므로 목적어 your
house 다음에 목적격 보어로 과거분사 remodeled가 와
야 알맞다.

16 「find+목적어+목적격 보어」(～이 …하는 것을 발견하다)
구문이다.

시험 직전에 챙겨 보는 비법노트   p. 20

한눈에 쏙!

2 1) have   2) let   3) see   4) watch   5) hear
    6) smell   7) feel   8) help

헷갈리지 말자!

1 happy   2 sleep
3 (to) contact   4 to wear

해설

1 목적격 보어로 형용사 happy가 알맞다.

2 사역동사 let은 목적격 보어로 동사원형 sleep이 알맞
다.

3 준사역동사 help는 목적격 보어로 동사원형이나 to부
정사가 알맞다.

4 ask는 목적격 보어로 to부정사가 알맞다.

CHAPTER 02
to부정사

03 용법, 의미상의 주어, 부정

Let's Check It Out   p. 23

A   1   부사적 용법(결과)
     2   명사적 용법(진주어)

     3   형용사적 용법(대명사 수식)
     4   부사적 용법(감정의 원인)

B   1   of → for   2   for → of
    3   we → us   4   for → of

C   1   never to tell   2   not to lose
    3   not to skip   4   not to wake up

D   1   dangerous to swim in
    2   in order to keep
    3   possible for me to
    4   wise of him to spend
    5   not to worry

Ready for Exams   p. 24

1   ③   2 ④

3   a piece of cake for me to raise

4   I am going to tell the guy not to call me again.

1 to부정사의 의미상의 주어가 'of+목적격'이므로 성품 형용
사가 와야 한다.

2 [보기]의 밑줄 친 to부정사는 부사적 용법(목적)으로 사용되
었다. ⓐ 부사적 용법(감정의 원인) ⓑ 부사적 용법(판단의 근
거) ⓒ 명사적 용법(pretend동사의 목적어) ⓓ 부사적 용법
(형용사 수식) ⓔ 명사적 용법(진주어 역할)

3 to부정사의 의미상의 주어는 일반 형용사일 경우 'for+목적
격'을 쓴다. a piece of cake는 명사이지만 very easy와
같은 의미로 볼 수 있다.

4 to부정사의 부정은 「not[never] to+동사원형」을 쓰는데 8
번째 단어가 3글자여야 하므로 not to ～로 쓴다.

04 시제, 독립부정사, 대부정사

Let's Check It Out   p. 26

A   1   seems / is   2   seemed / worked
    3   seems to be
    4   appeared to have attacked
    5   didn't seem to have lost

B   1   To be sure
    2   To tell (you) the truth
    3   To be frank[honest] (with you)
    4   Sad to say
    5   To begin with

C   1   You can stay here if you want to <u>stay here</u>.
    2   I can help her, but she never asks me to <u>help her</u>.
    3   A: Will you come to the party?
         B: Sure. I'd love to <u>go to the party</u>.

Ready for Exams

p. 27

1 ③   2 ①
3 You can drive my car if you want to.
4 help you whenever you want me to

해설

1 'seem to+동사원형'은 주절과 같은 시제이므로 copied로 써야 한다.

2 to부정사가 독립적으로 사용되어 문장 전체를 수식하도록 strangely를 strange로 고쳐야 한다. (독립부정사)

3 You can drive my car if you want to drive it.에서 to drive it을 대부정사로 쓴다. if가 6번째 어휘가 되도록 해야 하므로 주절을 먼저 써야 한다.

4 마지막 to 이하에 help you가 생략되어 있다. (대부정사)

Review Test

p. 28

01 ③   02 ④
03 ③   04 ② ④
05 ② ④ ⑤   06 ⑤
07 ③   08 ②
09 He came back to find his daughter sick in bed.
10 ⓐ for → of
11 ⓑ not to play ⓒ to 삭제 또는 to me
12 It was careless of him to touch
13 (1) It seems that she is diligent.
     (2) It seemed that she was diligent.
14 step on your foot
15 to make matters[things] worse
16 (1) not to make a mess
     (2) never to turn on the computer

해설

01 ③은 부사적 용법이고, [보기]와 나머지는 명사적 용법 이다.

02 성품 형용사는 의미상의 주어를 'of+목적격'으로 쓴다.

03 Be careful not to catch a cold.로 영작할 수 있다.

04 관심을 잃은 것이 주절의 시제인 현재보다 앞선 것이므로 완료부정사로 써야 한다. 따라서 Carmen seems to have lost interest in studying. (또는 It seems that Carmen lost interest in studying.)이 맞다.

05 종속절의 시제가 주절보다 앞선 시제로, 완료부정사를 써서 She appears to have been a doctor.로 전환할 수 있다.

06 '솔직히 말해서'에 해당하는 독립부정사는 To be frank[honest] (with you)이다.

07 decide는 to부정사를 목적어로 취하고, 내용상 가지 말라고 했으므로 not to go에서 공통어구 go alone을 생략할 수 있다.

08 ⓐ She → It ⓑ not visit → not to visit

09 '~한 결과 …하다'의 부사적 용법 중 결과 용법을 이용한다.

10 성품 형용사가 오면 'of+목적격'으로 의미상의 주어를 표현한다.

11 ⓑ ask A to B(A에게 B를 요청하다)에서 to B를 부정하므로 not to play로 써야 한다. ⓒ 공통된 부분이 없어 대부정사를 쓸 이유가 없으므로 삭제하면 된다.

12 '그가 젖은 손으로 플러그를 만진 것은 부주의했다'라는 의미의 문장이다. 성품 형용사(careless)는 'of+목적격'으로 to 부정사의 의미상의 주어를 쓴다.

13 단순부정사가 왔으므로 주절의 시제와 that절의 시제는 같다.

14 반복되는 어구를 쓰면 되는데, to 다음에는 동사원형을 써야 하므로 step으로 써야 한다.

15 독립부정사 to make matters[things] worse를 쓰면 된다. worse는 bad의 비교급이다.

16 to부정사의 부정은 「not[never] to+동사원형」으로 쓴다.

시험 직전에 챙겨 보는 비법노트

p. 30

한눈에 쏙!

1 1) 목적어   2) 보어   3) 형용사적   4) 원인
    5) 근거   6) 결과
2 1) for   2) 성품
3 1) 동사원형   2) have   3) p.p.

헷갈리지 말자!

1 to be   2 of
3 not to   4 to have made
5 to be sure

해설

1 '~해서 결국 …하다'의 의미인 to부정사의 결과적 용법에 해당하므로 to be로 써야 한다.

2 성품형용사의 부정사의 의미상의 주어는 「of+목적격」이므로 of로 고쳐야 한다.

3 to부정사의 부정형은 「not[never] to+동사원형」이므로 not to로 고쳐야 한다.

4 주절은 현재(seems)이고 종속절은 과거(made)이므로 완료부정사인 to have made로 고쳐야 한다.

5 '확실히'란 뜻의 독립부정사는 to be sure이다.

CHAPTER 03
동명사

UNIT 05 용법, 의미상의 주어, 부정

Let's Check It Out

p. 33

A 1 주어   2 전치사의 목적어
    3 보어   4 목적어
    5 주어

B　1　my 또는 me　　　2　her
　　3　his 또는 him　　　4　the tree
　　5　your 또는 you

C　1　not being　　　2　not having
　　3　never telling

D　1　sorry / suspecting
　　2　mad / my[me] leaving
　　3　Beginning / continuing
　　4　not listening to
　　5　falling / refusing

Ready for Exams　　　　p. 34

1　③　　　　　　　　　2　②
3　The students hated the teacher('s) nagging.
4　He is considering not going to work.

해설

1　[보기]와 ③은 보어로 쓰인 동명사이다. ① 전치사의 목적어
　②동사구의 목적어 ④ 주어 ⑤ 동사의 목적어

2　두 문장은 모두 문법적으로 옳은 문장이다. 동명사의 의미상
　의 주어로 목적격이 가능한 경우는 목적어 자리에 올 경우, 부
　정내명사, 무생물일 경우이다.

3　동명사(nagging)의 의미상의 주어는 the teacher이며, 소
　유격 또는 목적격 둘 다 가능하다.

4　월요일이라 일하러 가기 싫어서 결근을 할까 생각하는 그림
　이다. consider동사는 동명사를 목적어로 취한다. 동명사의
　부정은 'not+동명사'이다.

ⓊⓃⒾⓉ 06　동명사, 현재분사, to부정사

Let's Check It Out　　　　p. 36

A　1　eating / 동명사　　　2　talking / 현재분사
　　3　walking / 동명사　　4　waving / 현재분사
　　5　rising / 현재분사

B　1　doing　　　　　　　2　to see
　　3　to shout 또는 shouting
　　4　to visit　　　　　　5　to send

C　1　Aren't / tired of eating
　　2　couldn't help thinking
　　3　How about renting
　　4　felt like going back

D　1　to live　　　　　　2　wishing
　　3　being　　　　　　4　seeing

Ready for Exams　　　　p. 37

1　③　　　　　　　　　2　③
3　to enjoy → enjoying
4　It is no use crying for help.

해설

1　ⓐ는 용도, 목적을 나타내는 동명사이고, ⓓ는 전치사의 목적
　어로 쓰인 동명사이다.

2　give up+-ing이므로 ③이 어색하다. (to play → playing)
　②는 상황에 따라 asking 또는 to ask가 둘 다 가능하다.

3　과거의 일에 대해 '~한 것을 기억하다'라고 말할 때는
　remember -ing로 쓴다.

4　It is no use+-ing는 '~해봐야 소용없다'라는 의미의 관용
　적 표현이다.

Review Test　　　　p. 38

01　①　　　　　　　02　① ④
03　⑤　　　　　　　04　②
05　②　　　　　　　06　⑤
07　① ③　　　　　　08　②
09　The secretary's mistake was not locking the door.
10　being from Kenya
11　be no possibility of Minjun('s) winning
12　her for not arriving on time
13　ⓑ to sing → singing
14　(1) cooking → 현재분사
　　(2) cooking → 동명사
15　We felt like going back to the forest.
16　She tried to change the tires.
17　They are accustomed to swimming in the
　　sea[ocean].

해설

01　keep (on)은 동명사를 목적어로 취하므로 working이 맞고,
　전치사(without)의 목적어는 동명사를 써야 하므로 paying
　이 맞다.

02　전치사(about)의 목적어로는 동명사가 와야 하며, 의미상의
　주어는 소유격 또는 목적격으로 나타내야 한다.

03　① are → is ② mean → means ③ to 삭제
　④ help → helping

04　내용상 '나에게 이메일 보낼 것을 잊었다'이므로 'forget+to
　부정사'를 써야 한다.

05　②는 용도, 목적을 나타내는 동명사이고, 나머지는 현재분사
　이다.

06　③ look forward to 다음에는 동명사를 쓰므로 get이 아니
　라 getting이 필요하다. ① There is no inviting Rocky.
　② Clare is busy talking on the phone. ③ Rachel
　spent all her money on mirrors. ④ Jenna is not
　used to eating spicy ramen. ⑤ Zinna is looking
　forward to getting married.

07　① go → going ③ to wait → waiting

08　ⓓ와 ①는 to부정사를 목적어로 취한다.

09　lock을 보어로 쓰일 수 있는 동명사 형태로 고쳐야 하며, 동
　명사의 부정은 동명사 앞에 not을 쓴다.

10　전치사(of) 다음에는 동명사를 써서 표현한다.

11　「seem to+동사원형」은 동일한 시제에 관한 표현이다. 동
　명사의 의미상의 주어는 소유격 또는 목적격으로 나타낸다.

12　punished의 목적어로 her가 필요하고, 동명사의 부정은 동
　명사 앞에 not을 쓰며, 동명사의 의미상의 주어는 문장의 목

적어(her)이므로 쓸 필요가 없다.

13 dislike는 동명사만 목적어로 취한다.

14 (1) 명사(girl)를 꾸며주는 현재분사가 알맞다.
   (2) is의 주어로 쓰인 동명사이다.

15 feel like+-ing는 '~하고 싶다'라는 의미의 관용적 표현이다.

16 'try+to부정사'는 '~하려고 노력하다'이다.

17 '~하는 것에 익숙하다'라는 표현으로는 be used to+-ing와 be accustomed to+-ing가 있는데 3번째 단어를 a로 시작해야 한다고 했으므로 accustomed를 쓴다.

시험 직전에 챙겨 보는 비법노트   p. 40

한눈에 쏙!

1 1) 주어   2) 보어   3) 목적어   4) 전치사의 목적어
2 1) 목적   2) 동작
3 ① finish, enjoy, mind, give up, avoid, deny
  ② want, hope, wish, plan, agree, decide
  ③ Stop forgetting and try to remember before you regret!

헷갈리지 말자!

1 closing   2 His
3 never climbing
4 raining 또는 to rain

1 전치사(without) 다음에는 동명사인 closing으로 써야 한다.
2 동명사의 의미상의 주어는 목적격도 가능하지만 목적어 자리일 때이고 여기서는 주어 자리이므로 His로 고쳐야 한다.
3 동명사의 부정은 「not[never]+동명사」로 표현하므로 never climbing으로 고쳐야 한다.
4 start는 동명사와 to부정사를 둘 다 목적어로 취하므로 raining 또는 to rain으로 고쳐야 한다.

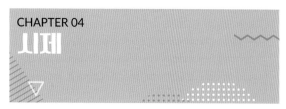

CHAPTER 04
시제

07 단순 시제, 현재완료 시제

Let's Check It Out   p. 43

A 1 goes   2 hit
  3 will be   4 is
  5 arrive   6 will arrive

B 1 have owned   2 has been
  3 has cleaned   4 didn't see
  5 has gone

C 1 will help → help   2 어색한 곳 없음
  3 drops → will drop
  4 since → for (또는 hours → hours ago)
  5 was → has been
  6 have gone → have been

Ready for Exams   p. 44

1 ④   2 ③ ④
3 The sun rises in the east and sets in the west.
4 has just missed the train

1 과거의 어느 시점부터 지금까지 진행 중인 상황은 현재완료 진행(have been+-ing)을 쓴다. yet은 부정문에서 '아직 ~ 않다'의 뜻이다. (하루 종일 비가 내리고 있고, 아직 멈추지 않았다.)
2 ⓐ 계속 ⓑ ⓔ 경험 ⓒ ⓓ 완료
3 불변의 진리는 현재 시제로 쓴다 현재 시제에서 주어가 3인칭 단수일 때 동사에 -s를 붙이는 것에 유의한다.
4 남자가 막 기차를 놓친 장면으로, 현재완료의 완료 용법을 쓰면 된다. (miss-missed-missed)

08 과거완료 시제, 진행 시제

Let's Check It Out   p. 46

A 1 had left   2 had lent
  3 had rained   4 had arrived

B 1 Were you shopping   2 has been playing
  3 have been learning   4 had been driving

C 1 is teaching   2 were running
  3 has sung   4 had lost
  5 has been snowing

Ready for Exams   p. 47

1 ③   2 ①
3 have been   4 had learned / moved

1 엄마가 드론을 사준 것이 내가 잃어버린 것보다 앞선 일이므로 과거완료 시제가 알맞다.
2 그들이 여기로 이사 온 과거 시점 이전에 10년 동안 결혼한 상태였으므로 과거완료 had been married가 알맞다.
3 과거의 시점부터 현재까지 계속되는 상황은 현재완료를 써서 나타낸다. (나는 쌍둥이 자매가 있다. 우리는 함께 태어났다. 우리는 여전히 함께이다. → 쌍둥이 자매와 나는 태어나면서부터 계속 함께 있어 왔다.)
4 보스턴으로 이사를 간 과거 시점 전에 10년 동안 영어 공부를

했었기 때문에 과거완료 had+p.p.를 쓴다.

Review Test

01 ②　　　　　　　　　　02 ④
03 ②　　　　　　　　　　04 ④
05 ③　　　　　　　　　　06 ⑤
07 ⑤　　　　　　　　　　08 ⑤
09 Tony resembles his mother.
10 has lived in Paris since last year
11 have been knowing → have known
12 ⓐ stays → will stay
13 will have taken
14 have been waiting
15 (A) had never drawn (B) had drawn

해설

01 현재의 습관 및 반복적 행위는 현재 시제로 나타낸다. (practice meditation: 명상을 하다)
02 ⓐ 조건절(if절)에서는 현재 시제가 미래의 뜻을 나타낸다. (will have → has) ⓒ just now(방금 전에)는 과거 부사이므로 현재완료와 쓸 수 없고 과거 시제로 써야 한다. (has finished → finished) ⓓ 불변의 진리는 현재로 쓴다. (froze → freezes)
03 ·현재완료 시제: have+p.p. (spread-spread-spread) (그 소문은 이미 학교에 퍼졌어.)
   ·get married: 결혼하다 (그들은 결국 결혼하지 않았다.)
04 John이 지금 여기 없으므로 현재완료의 결과 용법으로 표현한다.
05 ⓐ when은 현재완료와 함께 쓸 수 없고 단순 시제(현재, 과거, 미래)에 모두 쓰인다. (→ When did you go to Japan?) ⓑ 과거 부사(a week ago)가 있으므로 과거 시제로 써야 한다. (has met → met) ⓒ 현재완료 수동태로 어법상 올바른 문장이다
06 since는 현재완료 또는 현재완료 진행형에 쓰이므로 ⑤가 맞다.
07 8년 전부터 현재까지 계속되는지를 묻고 있으므로, 현재완료 진행(have/has been+-ing)이 알맞다.
08 시계를 잃어버린 것이 찾은 것(found)보다 먼저 일어났으므로, 과거완료(had+p.p.) 시제가 알맞다. (나는 어제 공원에서 내 시계를 잃어버렸다. 나는 오늘 그 시계를 찾았다. → 나는 공원에서 잃어버렸던 그 시계를 찾았다.)
09 resemble(닮다)동사는 항상 변하지 않는 사실이므로 현재형을 쓴다. (Tony는 어머니를 닮았다.)
10 과거 시점(last year)부터 현재까지 이어지는 동작이므로 현재완료의 계속 용법에 해당한다. 현재완료 진행형도 쓸 수 있지만 단어 수에 어긋난다.
11 인식을 나타내는 know(알다) 동사는 진행형으로 쓸 수 없으므로 현재완료 진행이 아니라 현재완료로 쓰는 것이 알맞다.
12 ⓐ if절이 부사절이 아니라 wonder의 목적어인 명사절이므로 미래 시제로 미래를 표현해야 한다. ⓑ if절이 부사절이므로 현재 시제를 쓴 것이 올바르다.
13 현재부터 미래 시점까지 계속되는 일을 나타내는 미래완료 (will have+p.p.)를 써야 한다.
14 30분 전에 시작된 동작이 현재까지 계속되고 있으므로, 현재

완료 진행(have been+-ing)을 써서 '~해 오고 있는 중이다'라는 의미를 표현한다. (A: 안녕하세요. 여기서 뭐하고 계세요? B: 매니저를 만나려고 기다리는 중입니다. 저는 30분 동안 기다리고 있어요.)
15 둘 다 과거 시제보다 더 과거의 일이므로, 과거완료가 알맞다. ("저, 양 한 마리만 그려 줘⋯" 나는 어린 왕자에게 그림을 그릴 줄 모른다고 말했다. 그는 나에게 말했다. "괜찮아. 양 한 마리만 그려 줘⋯" 그러나 나는 양을 그려 본 적이 없었다. 그래서 나는 내가 그토록 자주 그렸던 두 가지 그림 중에서 하나를 그에게 그려주었다. 그것은 보아 뱀 속에 들어 있는 코끼리였다.)

시험 직전에 챙겨 보는 비법노트

한눈에 쏙!

1 1) was/were　2) be　3) 미래
2 1) has/have+p.p.　2) been

헷갈리지 말자!

1 went　　　　　　　　2 has
3 had studied

해설

1 last year 명백한 과거 부사가 있으므로 시제는 과거형 went가 알맞다
2 소유동사 have는 진행형을 쓰지 않으므로 주어 My sister에 알맞은 현재형 has가 알맞다.
3 before I started 과거 시제 이전의 의미를 나타내는 대과거형 'had+과거분사형'이 알맞다.

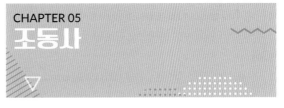

CHAPTER 05
조동사

조동사(1)

Let's Check It Out

A 1 need not　　　　　2 isn't going to
　 3 ought not to　　　4 cannot / rest

B 1 can't be sick
　 2 may not make any noise
　 3 cannot listen to / without falling asleep
　 4 may well say
　 5 cannot be too careful

C 1 ought　　　　　　2 should
　 3 should　　　　　 4 should
　 5 should

1 ⑤   2 ① ⑤
3 ought not to
4 We insisted that he admit his mistake.

해설

1 ⓔ는 '허락'이고 나머지는 '추측'이다.
2 필요를 나타내는 necessary 다음의 that절에는
「(should)+동사원형」이 온다.
3 should not은 ought not to와 유사한 의미이다.
4 주장 동사 insist 다음에 오는 that절에서 조동사 should는
생략할 수 있다.

조동사(2)

Let's Check It Out   p. 56

A   1 had better take   2 used to be
    3 would like to meet

B   1 to go → go   2 as → than
    3 had not better → had better not
    4 swim → swimming (또는 am 삭제)
    5 stealing → steal

C   1 should   2 must
    3 cannot   4 might

Ready for Exams   p. 57

1 ④   2 ①
3 ⓐ had not better → had better not
4 (A) You should have taken your umbrella.
   (B) I should have listened to you.

해설

1 '~하곤 했다'라는 과거의 습관을 나타내므로 「used to+동
사원형」을 쓴다.
2 '그 아이들은 무척 예의가 바랐다. 그들은 교육을 잘 받았음에
틀림없다'라는 의미가 되어야 자연스럽다. (must have+
p.p.: ~였음에 틀림없다)
3 had better의 부정은 had better not이다.
4 '~했어야 했다'는 과거에 대한 후회는 should have+p.p.
로 나타낸다.

Review Test   p. 58

01 ④ ⑤   02 ②
03 ③   04 ①
05 ④   06 ① ④
07 ①   08 ②
09 You must not ride your bike
10 We didn't have[need] to argue about it then.
11 Such things ought not to be allowed.

12 The doctor suggested that I (should) drink a lot
    of water.
13 I may as well skip dinner as eat the cold pizza.
14 You may as well stop smoking.
15 It's a pity that Beauty should marry the beast.
16 should have focused
17 The soap opera is so sad that I would not like to
    watch it again.

해설

01 상대방의 허락을 구해야 하느냐는 A의 질문에 B가 원하는 대
로 할 수 있다고 했으므로, 빈칸에는 불필요를 나타내는 응답
이 알맞다.
02 '~하는 것이 좋겠다'는 충고, 조언의 의미를 갖는 had
better가 알맞다.
03 didn't use는 다음에 to가 와야 used to의 부정문이 된다.
04 주절에 essential이 있는 문장의 that절에는 「(should)+
동사원형」이 와야 한다.
05 ⓑ suggest (that)+주어+(should)+동사원형 (eats →
eat) ⓒ may[might] well+동사원형: ~하는 것이 당연하
다 (saving → save)
06 might[may] have+p.p.: ~했을지도 모른다 (그 범죄자는
절에 숨었을지도 모른다.)
07 would rather+동사원형(+than+동사원형): (…하느니)
~하는 게 더 낫다
08 cannot help+-ing = cannot but+동사원형: ~하지 않
을 수 없다
09 내용상 자전거를 타면 안 된다는 금지의 표현으로 must not
을 이용한다. don't have to는 '~할 필요가 없다'이다.
10 '~할 필요 없다'는 의미의 don't have to를 과거 시제로 써
야 하므로 didn't have[need] to가 알맞다.
11 ought to의 부정은 ought not to이다.
12 suggest동사가 있는 문장의 that절에는 「(should)+동사
원형」이 와야 한다.
13 may[might] as well A(동사원형) as B(동사원형): B 하
기보다는 A 하는 편이 낫다
14 may as well = had better: ~하는 게 낫다
15 It's a pity that+주어+(should)+동사원형: ~해야 하는
것은 안타까운 일이다
16 should have p.p.는 '~했어야 했다'는 뜻으로, 과거에 이
루지 못한 일에 대한 후회를 나타낸다. (나는 시험에 집중했어
야 했다.)
17 would not like to는 '~하고 싶지 않다'라는 의미를 나타낸
다.

시험 직전에 챙겨 보는 비법노트   p. 60

한눈에 쏙!

1   1) 동사원형
2   1) ~하면 안 된다   2) must   3) ~할 필요 없다
    4) have   5) need
3   1) but   2) ~하지 않을 수 없다   3) may as well
    4) ~하는 편이 낫다   5) be   6) ~했어야 했다
    7) ~했음에 틀림없다   8) should   9) 동사원형

헷갈리지 말자!

1 don't have[need] to 또는 need not
2 couldn't help having
3 had better not

해설

1 must not은 '~하면 안 된다'의 금지이고 don't have to는 '~할 필요 없다'의 불필요 의무이므로 의미상 불필요의 대답이 알맞다.

2 can't help+-ing '~하지 않을 수 없다'의 중요 표현으로 동명사형 having이 알맞다.

3 had better는 조동사로 다음에 not이 오는 것이 알맞다. (had better not: ~하지 않는 게 낫겠다)

CHAPTER 06
수동태

UNIT 11 조동사, 진행형, 완료형의 수동태

Let's Check It Out
p. 63

A 1 is loved
   2 speak
   3 was written
   4 aren't answered
   5 were loved

B 1 should not be forgotten
   2 being washed
   3 has been composed
   4 can[can't] live
   5 had been placed

C 1 is being played
   2 won't be used
   3 are constructing
   4 has never been accepted
   5 had been lost

Ready for Exams
p. 64

1 ④
2 ④
3 The prisoners are being released now.
4 (1) has / been dropped
   (2) is broken

해설

1 편지가 보내진 것이므로 수동태로 써야 하며, 과거 부사 last week가 있으므로 시제는 과거로 쓴다.

2 Those dogs can[may, might] be adopted as pets by Justin.으로 영작할 수 있다.

3 진행형의 수동태 기본형은 be being+p.p.이며 by them은 생략할 수 있다.

4 (1) 현재완료 수동태 has been dropped를 쓴다.

(2) 현재 부서져 있는 상태이므로 is broken으로 써야 한다.

UNIT 12 여러 가지 수동태

Let's Check It Out
p. 66

A 1 My hair was cut too short
   2 am made hungry by
   3 He was elected chairman
   4 He was called "the crazy guy"
   5 was advised to work out

B 1 to wash
   2 어색한 곳 없음
   3 to participate
   4 어색한 곳 없음

C 1 of by
   2 up by
   3 is believed
   4 She
   5 with

D 1 wasn't taken care of
   2 are said to make

Ready for Exams
p. 67

1 ③
2 ③
3 (1) was thought
   (2) that
   (3) The movie / to be
4 was turned off

해설

1 목적어 her house가 수동태의 주어가 되어야 하며, 인칭, 수, 시제에 맞도록 be동사는 was가 알맞다.

2 He made the boys clean the tables.가 능동태 문장이다. 수동태에서는 clean 앞에 to를 써야 한다.

3 that절이 목적어인 경우의 수동태이다. That절을 주어로 → 'by+일반인' 생략 → 가주어-진주어 구문 → that절의 주어를 문장 주어로 전환하면 된다.

4 동사구의 수동태는 한 덩어리로 인식하여 전환하고 마지막 전치사에 주의한다. (Joan과 Ken은 도서관에서 공부하고 있었다. Joan은 간식을 좀 사러 밖에 나갔고, Kon은 계속 공부를 했다. 갑자기 Joan의 전화벨이 울리기 시작했다. Ken은 당황했다. 그는 즉시 전화기 전원을 껐다.)

Review Test
p. 68

01 ⑤
02 ④
03 ⑤
04 ①
05 ②
06 ⑤
07 ②
08 ② ③
09 Y A C H T
10 The dogs had to be walked by her.
11 is not being paid attention to (by the students)
12 ⓑ cooked ⓒ Was it enjoyed
13 (1) is believed that the grizzly bear is the scariest

animal

(2) is believed to be the scariest animal

14 The man's wig was taken off by the monkey.

15 Guzal was made to stop her car by the police officer.

해설

01 'ought to+동사원형'의 수동태는 ought to be+p.p.이므로 This problem ought to be solved by you.로 영작할 수 있다.

02 조동사의 수동태는 「조동사+be+p.p.」이다.

03 테니스 경기가 7월부터 취소되어 온 것이므로 수동을 의미하는 have been+p.p. 형태의 현재완료 수동태가 알맞다.

04 5형식 부정문의 수동태로, be allowed to ~에서 not을 be 다음에 쓰면 된다.

05 They think that the construction is going to be finished next month.의 수동태이다.

06 be being+p.p.는 진행형의 수동태이고 'by+불필요한 행위자(someone)'가 생략된 문장이다.

07 ⓑ move → to move ⓓ done → be done

08 지각동사(watch)의 수동태에서 목적격 보어는 to부정사 또는 -ing 형태가 된다.

09 올바른 문장인 ⓑ의 Y ⓒ의 A ⓓ의 T를 배열해서 넣으면 된다. (ⓐ laughed → laughed at ⓔ saying → said)

10 have to도 조동사의 범주에 속하므로 「조동사+be+p.p.」 형태로 바꾸면 된다.

11 선생님이 주어이므로 수동태로 써야 하며, 동사구의 수동태는 한 덩어리로 인식해서 전환한다.

12 ⓑ 주체가 you이므로 능동태로 써야 한다. ⓒ it은 carbonara를 말하므로 수동태인 Was it enjoyed로 써야 한다.

13 (1)은 가주어-진주어 구문으로 전환한 것이고 (2)는 that절의 주어를 문장의 주어로 전환한 것이다.

14 The monkey took off the man's wig.의 수동태로, 동사구 take off를 한 덩어리로 인식하여 전환한다.

15 The police officer made Guzal stop her car.를 수동태 문장으로 전환하면 된다. 이때 stop 앞에 to를 써야 하는 것에 유의한다.

시험 직전에 챙겨 보는 비법노트 p. 70

한눈에 쏙!

1 1) be 2) p.p. 3) be 4) being 5) p.p.
6) have/has 7) been 8) p.p.

2 1) to 2) 동사원형 3) to 4) 동사원형 5) to 6) 동사원형 7) -ing

3 1) 나머지 동사구 2) by 3) is said that
4) is said to

헷갈리지 말자!

1 was being destroyed

2 had never been worn

3 entering 또는 to enter

해설

1 진행형의 수동태는 「be+being+p.p.」이므로

destroyed로 고쳐야 한다.

2 과거완료형의 수동태는 「had been+p.p.」이므로 been worn으로 고쳐야 한다.

3 지각동사의 수동태는 「be+지각동사(p.p.)+-ing 또는 to+동사원형」이므로 entering 또는 to enter로 고쳐야 한다.

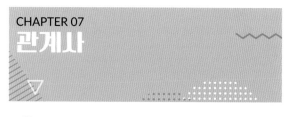

CHAPTER 07
관계사

UNIT 13 관계대명사의 역할과 용법

Let's Check It Out p. 73

A 1 who(m) 또는 that 2 who 또는 that
3 which 4 who 또는 that
5 what 6 which

B 1 whose mother is
2 whose functions are simple
3 which[that] I bought for her / what I bought for her
4 which I've read seven times

C 1 that 2 what
3 What 4 that
5 what

Ready for Exams p. 74

1 ④ 2 ②
3 who
4 What I want to know is her phone number.

해설

1 ·뒤에 관사 없는 주어가 있으므로 소유격 관계대명사가 알맞다.
·look up to의 목적어 역할을 하는 목적격 관계대명사가 와야 하며, 선행사가 사람(a teacher)이므로 who(m) 또는 that이 알맞다.

2 ⓐ 관계대명사 다음에 동사 lived가 왔으므로 주격 who가 알맞다. ⓒ 관계대명사 다음에 명사가 왔으므로 소유격 whose가 알맞다.

3 관계대명사의 계속적 용법은 '접속사+주어'와 같은 의미이다. 선행사가 사람이고 주격이므로 who로 쓴다. that은 계속적 용법으로 쓸 수 없다.

4 선행사를 포함한 관계대명사 what을 넣어야 9단어로 쓸 수 있다.

⑭ 관계부사, 관계사의 생략

Let's Check It Out
p. 76

A 1 when   2 why
   3 How   4 where

B 1 (1) which 또는 that / at
     (2) at which
     (3) where
   2 (1) which 또는 that
     (2) on which
     (3) when

C 1 She will keep the ring which[that] she got from her grandmother.
   2 The book which[that] he read yesterday was about a missing child.
   3 The man who[that] was attacked by some strangers is in the hospital now.
   4 The pizza which[that] was baked in the oven was tasty.
   5 He was the first man that[who(m)] I loved.

Ready for Exams
p. 77

1 ①⑤   2 ③⑤
3 The man (who was) satisfied with the product ordered another one.
4 (1) how he earned the money
   (2) the way he earned the money

해설

1 ① 문장 끝에 전치사가 있는데 관계부사 where를 쓸 수 없다. 전치사를 없애거나 where를 which로 바꾸어야 한다. ⑤ 주어가 the house로 단수이므로 동사는 has가 알맞다.
2 ⓑ the day가 뒤 문장에서 on the day로 쓰이므로 관계부사 when을 써야 한다. ⓒ 보어절을 이끄는 접속사 that이 알맞다.
3 「주격 관계대명사+be동사」는 같이 생략 가능하다. 둘 중 하나만 생략할 수는 없다.
4 방법은 the way 또는 how를 써서 표현하고, 둘이 같이 쓸 수는 없다.

⑮ 복합관계사

Let's Check It Out
p. 79

A 1 Whichever   2 Whatever
   3 whoever   4 whomever

B 1 whatever   2 Whoever
   3 However   4 whatever
   5 Whenever

C 1 Whenever you need my help
   2 Wherever he goes
   3 No matter how smart
   4 anything that you want

Ready for Exams
p. 80

1 ①   2 ④
3 Whatever
4 Wherever he appeared / a crowd gathered

해설

1 whatever는 '무엇을 ～하더라도'라는 뜻으로 양보의 부사절을 이끈다. (네가 무슨 말을 해도 나는 너를 용서하지 않을 것이다.)
2 ④는 '어디든지'라는 의미의 Wherever가 알맞고, 나머지는 '～할 때마다'라는 의미의 Whenever가 알맞다.
3 no matter what (= whatever): '무엇이든지' (네가 무엇을 선택하든, 난 상관없다.)
4 wherever는 복합관계부사로 양보절을 이끈다.
(wherever = no matter where: '어디에서 ～하든지')

Review Test
p. 81

01 ③   02 ①③⑤
03 ⑤   04 ②
05 ③   06 ④
07 ①   08 ①
09 ②   10 ⑤
11 ①   12 ①
13 ④   14 ①④
15 ①⑤
16 The boy whose sister is a diplomat wants to study politics.
17 and I went to elementary school with him
18 the boy who[that] helped
19 how 또는 the way
20 where
21 matter what your idea is
22 Minji has a crush on the boy running on the track.

해설

01 반복되는 명사인 선행사 a man이 뒤 문장에서 소유격으로 쓰였으므로 whose가 알맞다.
02 ⓐ him이 앞의 선행사 a friend이므로 삭제해야 한다. ⓑ 선행사가 everything이므로 that을 주로 쓰는 것이 맞다. ⓒ 주어가 the old lady이므로 동사는 lives이다. ⓓ who는 '누가'라는 의미의 의문사로 사용되었다. ⓔ who는 son과 연결하는 소유격 whose가 되어야 한다.
03 소유격 관계대명사는 생략할 수 없다.
04 ②의 which는 앞에 나온 영화를 가리키지만, 나머지는 앞 문장 전체를 가리킨다.
05 ③의 that은 '～라는 것을'로 해석되는 목적절을 이끄는 접속사이고, 나머지는 명사 다음에 쓰여 '～한'으로 해석되는 관계대명사이다.

06 관계대명사 앞에 전치사가 올 경우에는 관계대명사 that을 쓸 수 없다. (동해는 내가 태어난 도시이다.)

07 the day가 그 다음 문장에서 on the day로 쓰였으므로 관계부사 when(= on which)이 알맞다.

08 anything that은 whatever로 바꾸어 쓸 수 있다. (네가 필요한 어떤 것이든지 가져라.)

09 반복되는 명사 disease가 뒤 문장에서 전치사 about의 목적격으로 쓰였으므로 which가 알맞다. 관계대명사 that은 전치사 about 다음에 쓰일 수 없다. (be worried about: ~에 대해 걱정하다)

10 ⑤는 선행사 the park가 뒤 문장에서 부사의 자리로 in the park로 쓰여야 문장이 자연스러우므로 빈칸에 관계부사 where가 필요하고, 나머지는 관계대명사 목적격이 적절하다.

11 ① 주어진 문장과 같이 관계대명사 목적격 that[which]이 생략되어 있다. ② the bag (which was) made로 '관계대명사 주격+be동사'가 생략되어 있다. ③ The man (who is) looking ~으로 '관계대명사 주격+be동사'가 생략되어 있다. ④ that girl (who is) smiling ~으로 '관계대명사 주격+be동사' 생략 ⑤ I believe 다음에 목적절을 이끄는 접속사 that이 생략되어 있다.

12 '먼저 오는 사람은 누구든 제일 좋은 자리를 얻는다.'로 해석되며 whoever는 '~하는 사람은 누구든'으로 해석되는 명사절을 이끄는 복합관계대명사로 단수 취급한다.

13 ④의 what은 '무엇'으로 해석되는 의문사이고, 주어진 문장과 나머지 문장의 what은 '~하는 것'으로 해석되는 관계사이다.

14 주어진 문장과 ①, ④의 that은 '~하는'으로 해석되는 목적격 관계대명사이다. ②, ③, ⑤의 that은 '~라는 것, ~라고'로 해석되는 접속사이다.

15 ② 선행사가 사람이므로 which가 아닌 that[who]여야 한다. ③ 목적격 관계대명사 that이 알맞다. ④ 시간의 관계부사 when이 알맞다.

16 선행사가 사람인 소유격 관계대명사는 「whose+명사」의 순서로 쓴다.

17 계속적 용법으로 쓰인 관계대명사는 '접속사+대명사'로 바꿀 수 있다. 여기서 접속사는 내용상 and가 적절하다. with whom은 목적격 with him으로 바꾸어 문장의 원래 자리에 놓는다.

18 소년이 도와준 것이므로 주격 관계대명사 who 또는 that을 쓴다.

19 방법을 나타낼 때는 the way 또는 관계부사 how 둘 중 하나만 쓴다.

20 ·선행사가 Lima로 장소이므로 장소의 관계부사 where가 알맞다. (그녀는 먼저 리마로 가서 노인들을 돕는 훈련을 받았다.)
 ·'그들의 부모가 어디에 있는지'이므로 의문사 where가 알맞다. (그들은 집도 없었고, 자신들의 부모가 어디에 있는지조차 몰랐다.)

21 「접속사+주어+동사」의 어순이 알맞다. no matter what(무엇이든지)은 whatever와 같은 표현으로, 양보의 부사절을 이끈다. (A: 여름 방학을 보낼 방법에 대해 어떤 생각이 있니? B: 아니, 없어. 네가 무슨 생각을 가지고 있든지, 나는 그것에 동의해.)

22 관계대명사를 쓰지 말라고 했으므로 running 앞에 who [that] is를 생략해야 한다.

시험 직전에 챙겨 보는 비법노트 p. 84

한눈에 쏙!

1 1) very   2) only   3) same
2 1) 주   2) be   3) 관계부사
3 1) no matter   2) whatever

헷갈리지 말자!

1 which   2 what
3 the way 또는 how

해설

1 관계사 that은 전치사와 나란히 쓰일 수 없으므로 선행사 the subject 사물에 맞는 관계사 which가 알맞다.

2 I really want to get에서 목적어가 없고 that 앞에 선행사의 명사형이 없으므로 the thing which[that]의 뜻인 what이 알맞다.

3 the way와 how는 함께 쓰일 수 없고 둘 중 하나만 써야 한다.

CHAPTER 08
비교 구문

UNIT 16 비교 변화, 원급 이용 비교 구문

Let's Check It Out p. 87

A 1 better / best   2 worse / worst
   3 less / least   4 farther / farthest
   5 further / furthest   6 later / latest
   7 latter / last

B 1 would rather / than   2 farther
   3 rather than   4 senior[superior] to

C 1 worse than   2 less / is not
   3 longer than   4 we could

Ready for Exams p. 88

1 ②   2 ① ④
3 (1) four / more (2) as much (3) more than

해설

1 ·as ~ as...: 원급 비교
 ·'팀에서 가장 빠른 선수이다'가 알맞다.

2 '사람들은 내 언니가 나보다 훨씬 키가 작기 때문에 나보다 어리다고 생각한다.' 또는 '사람들은 내 여동생이 나보다 훨씬 키가 크게 때문에 나보다 나이가 많다고 생각한다.'가 적절하다.

3 (1) 아시아인들은 신흥 국가 사람들보다 4배 많이 SF 게임을 즐긴다.
(2) 미국인들은 아시아인들만큼 많이 SF 게임을 하지 않는다.
(3) 미국인들은 유럽인들보다 더 많이 SF 게임을 즐긴다.

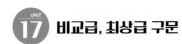

17 비교급, 최상급 구문

Let's Check It Out
p. 90

A 1 the faster 2 more brilliant
3 the most boring 4 the earlier
5 tools 6 the perfect

B 1 more precious than any
2 No other 3 the most diverse
4 There is / more generous

C 1 The more / the more arrogant
2 less and less
3 all the better because

Ready for Exams
p. 91

1 ① 2 ③
3 (1) The lower / the darker
(2) As / lower / darker

해설

1 ①은 '코끼리는 지상에서 다른 동물만큼 크지 않다.'는 뜻으로 최상급의 의미가 아니다. 주어진 문장과 나머지는 모두 코끼리가 지상에서 가장 큰 동물이라는 최상급의 의미를 나타낸다.

2 ⓐ in us → of us ⓑ more → the more ⓒ coin → coins

3 The+비교급+주어+동사 ~, the+비교급+주어+동사
= As+주어+동사+비교급 ~, 주어+동사+비교급 …: ~하면 할수록 더 …하다 (우리가 바다 밑으로 더 낮게 내려갈수록 점점 더 어두워진다.)

Review Test
p. 92

01 ③ 02 ④
03 ④ 04 ⑤
05 ① 06 ③
07 ③
08 Philip isn't as intelligent as Jack.
09 Jenny is one of the most brilliant students in my class.
10 (1) five times as expensive as
(2) five times more expensive than

11 growing more and more
12 you practice taekwondo / the better you will get at it
13 the highest / mountains
14 the more beautiful of the two
15 (1) is more difficult to climb than any other mountain
(2) No other mountain is more difficult to climb

해설

01 「not as+원급+as+비교 대상」은 「less+비교급+than+ 비교 대상」과 바꿔 쓸 수 있다.

02 would rather A than B(B보다 A 하는 것이 낫다)에서 A와 B에는 동사원형이 와야 한다. prefer A to B(B보다 A를 더 좋아하다)에서는 A와 B의 형태가 무엇이든 같은 형태로 비교하면 된다. rather than은 '~보다 오히려'의 의미이다.

03 the+서수+최상급+단수 명사: ~번째로 …한

04 ⑤는 '태평양은 다른 대양만큼 넓다'라는 의미이고, 나머지는 '태평양은 가장 넓은 대양이다'라는 의미의 최상급 표현이다.

05 ⓐ → She reads as many books as I do.
ⓑ → He studies twice as hard as you.

06 you spend much의 비교급은 you spend more이다. the more가 문장 앞에 나오고 you spend는 그 뒤에 쓴다. (the+비교급+주어+동사, the+비교급+주어+동사: ~하면 할수록 더욱 …하다)

07 남학생들이 두 번째로 선호하는 운동은 야구가 아니라 농구이다.

08 비교급을 동등 비교의 부정문으로 바꾸는 문제이다. (B~ 비교급+than A = A ~ not as[so] 원급+as B: A는 B만큼 ~하지 않다)

09 one of the+최상급+복수 명사: 가장 ~한 … 중 하나

10 구슬 10개와 연필 2개의 값이 같으므로 연필의 값이 구슬 값의 5배이다. 배수사 뒤에 비교급이나 원급을 써서 표현한다.

11 '점점 ~해지다'의 뜻으로 칸수에 맞게 growing으로, distant의 비교급은 more distant이므로 more and more를 쓰면 된다.

12 the+비교급+주어+동사 ~, the+비교급+주어+동사 …
= As+주어+동사+비교급 ~, 주어+동사+비교급: ~하면 할수록 더욱 …하다 (네가 태권도 연습을 더 많이 하면 할수록 너는 그것에 더 능숙해질 것이다.)

13 백두산이 가장 높으므로 최상급 the highest를 쓰고, 「of+복수 명사(mountains)」를 쓴다.

14 beautiful의 비교급은 more beautiful이고, of the two가 뒤에 오면 비교급 앞에 the를 쓴다.

15 「A ~ 비교급+than any other+단수 명사」 = 「No (other)+단수 명사 ~ 비교급+than A」는 모두 의미상 최상급을 나타내는 표현이다.

시험 직전에 챙겨 보는 비법노트
p. 94

한눈에 쏙!

1 1) bad 2) ill 3) little
2 1) superior 2) to
3 1) ~하면 할수록 점점 더 …하다 2) 원급
3) 비교급 4) than 5) any other

헷갈리지 말자!

1 the last   2 to
3 The more

 해설

1 최상급 last 앞에는 the를 써야 알맞다.
2 inferior to '~보다 열등한'은 비교의 의미이지만 that 대신에 to을 써야 한다.
3 the 비교급~, the＋비교급…: ~하면 할수록, 점점 더 …하다

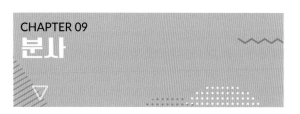

CHAPTER 09
분사

18 분사

Let's Check It Out
p. 97

A
1 excited   2 dancing
3 singing   4 used
5 spoken

B
1 interested   2 crying
3 exciting   4 disappointed
5 waiting

C
1 현   2 동
3 현   4 동
5 현

D
1 surprising   2 surprised
3 boring   4 bored
5 moving   6 moved
7 sleeping   8 sleeping

Ready for Exams
p. 98

1 ④   2 ⑤
3 ⑤
4 He was surprised at[by] the scene.

해설

1 첫 번째 빈칸은 집들이 부서진 것이므로 수동의 의미를 갖는 과거분사 destroyed가 알맞다. 두 번째 빈칸은 사람들이 울고 있으므로 능동의 의미를 갖는 현재분사 crying이 알맞다.
2 문맥상 '불타고 있는 태양'이라는 의미이므로 burn을 현재분사 burning으로 고쳐야 한다.
3 ① ② ③ ④ 현재분사 ⑤ 동명사

---

4 주어인 He가 놀란 것이므로 과거분사 surprised를 써야 한다. be surprised와 함께 사용되는 전치사는 at 또는 by이다.

19 분사구문

Let's Check It Out
p.100

A
1 Seeing   2 Not feeling
3 Watching TV
4 My father being busy

B
1 Feeling   2 Not living
3 Having stayed   4 being
5 running

C
1 Eating   2 어색한 곳 없음
3 serving (또는 and they served)
4 Having been born (또는 Born)

Ready for Exams
p. 101

1 ②   2 ④
3 (A) were dancing
  (B) with their eyes closed

해설

1 주어가 같고 시제가 같으므로 접속사를 생략하고 -ing를 붙이면 된다.
2 After she had been found ~의 분사구문으로, Having been found로 전환하며 Having been은 생략 가능하다.
3 (A) '춤을 추고 있었다'는 의미의 과거 진행형으로 were dancing이 알맞다.
  (B) 「with＋목적어＋분사」에서 눈이 감긴 것이므로 과거분사 closed로 써야 한다.

Review Test
p. 102

01 ④   02 ②
03 ③   04 ③
05 ②   06 ④
07 ④   08 ③
09 Look at the window broken by the ball.
10 Don't be late for the concert starting at 4.
11 I was rather disappointed with[by] his behavior.
12 smiling frog drawn
13 Not having time
14 Opening the window, she sneaked out to see her boyfriend.
15 ⓑThere being neither taxis nor buses, we had to walk back home. (또는 Because[As, Since] there were neither taxis nor buses, we had to walk back home.)
16 with her dog following her
17 living → lived / moving → to move

01 schedule과 fill은 수동의 관계이고, fill은 schedule을 수식하는 형용사의 역할을 해야 하므로 빈칸에는 과거분사 filled가 알맞다. (나는 숙제가 너무 많아. 숙제로 가득 찬 내 스케줄을 봐.)

02 '서 있는 소녀'이므로 stood가 아니라 현재분사 standing이 되어야 한다. (→ Look at the girl (who is) standing behind him.)

03 내가 그 뉴스에 놀란 것이므로 과거분사를 써야 한다. (shocking → shocked)

04 left의 주체가 you이므로 '남겨지다'라는 수동의 의미를 갖도록 If you are left alone at home으로 써야 한다. 과거분사 앞에 Being이 생략된 분사구문이다.

05 ① ③ ④ ⑤ 동명사 ② 현재분사

06 거의 50년 동안 산 것이 앞선 시제이고 내용상 이유가 되므로, Since[As, Because] she has lived 또는 분사구문 Having lived가 적절하다.

07 If we consider her age의 비인칭 독립분사구문으로 ④ 가 적절하다.

08 ⓑ It → It being ⓒ Arrived → Arriving
ⓔ Disappointing → Disappointed

09 창문이 깨진 것이므로 수동의 의미를 나타내는 과거분사 broken을 써야 한다.

10 starting at 4는 the concert를 꾸며주는 현재분사구이므로 the concert 뒤에 위치해야 한다.

11 실망을 당한 것이므로 수동의 의미를 나타내는 과거분사 disappointed를 써야 한다.

12 컵에 그려진 개구리가 미소 짓고 있으므로 빈칸에는 smiling frog drawn이 알맞다.

13 분사구문의 부정은 not+-ing ~로 표현한다.

14 '창문을 열고서 그녀는 남자친구를 만나기 위해 몰래 나갔다.' 라는 의미인데 접속사가 없으므로 분사(opening)로 문장을 시작하면 된다.

15 접속사가 없으므로 접속사를 추가해서 쓰거나 분사구문으로 써야 한다. 내용상 이유를 나타내는 접속사가 적절하다.

16 「with+목적어+분사」에서 강아지가 따라가는 것이므로 능동의 현재분사를 써야 한다.

17 이사를 원하지 않은 것보다 고향에 산 것이 앞선 시제이므로 having+p.p.로 써야 한다. want동사는 to부정사를 목적어로 취한다.

시험 직전에 챙겨 보는 비법노트   p. 104

한눈에 쏙!
1 1) 형용사
2 1) boring   2) bored
3 1) Having   2) nothing

헷갈리지 말자!
1 wearing   2 grazing
3 Surprised
4 Seen → Seeing 또는 Having seen / depressing → depressed
5 folded

---

1 The man이 wear하는 능동·진행이므로 wearing으로 고쳐야 한다.

2 '풀을 뜯고 있는 소'이므로 능동의 현재분사형이 알맞다.

3 문장의 주어 we가 뉴스에 놀래지는 수동의 의미를 갖는 과거분사형이 알맞다.

4 문장의 주어 I가 영화를 본 것이므로 능동의 의미를 갖는 현재분사형 Seeing이 되어야 하고, 내가 우울해진 것이므로 과거분사형 depressed가 알맞다.

5 「with+목적어+분사」 구문으로 목적어와 분사의 관계가 수동이므로 folded로 고쳐야 한다.

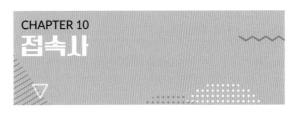

CHAPTER 10
접속사

UNIT 20 등위 접속사, 상관 접속사, 종속 접속사

Let's Check It Out   p. 107

A 1 had lunch   2 and
   3 or   4 skating
   5 and

B 1 neither → either (또는 or → nor)
   2 intelligence → intelligent
   3 love → loves
   4 If → Whether

C 1 if 또는 whether   2 if 또는 whether
   3 neither / nor   4 not only / but also
   5 It / that

Ready for Exams   p. 108

1 ③   2 ③
3 A bridge as well as houses was destroyed.
4 wants neither to eat snacks nor to drink yogurt

1 내용상 둘 다 작가가 아니라고 해야 하므로 neither A nor B를 쓴다.

2 ⓐ or → nor ⓒ are → is (either는 단수를 의미)

3 not only A but also B = B as well as A(A뿐만 아니라 B도)에서 동사는 B에 일치시킨다. (집들뿐만 아니라 다리도 파괴되었다.)

4 neither A nor B(A도 B도 아니다) 구문을 쓴다. to eat와 to drink를 병렬 구조로 쓰는 것에 유의한다.

21 종속 접속사

Let's Check It Out
p. 110

A
1 Although   2 before
3 As   4 while
5 unless   6 because of
7 although   8 such a

B
1 so tired that I couldn't
2 so / that   3 so that
4 in order not to (또는 so that you won't[don't],
so as not to)

C
1 ~하기 때문에   2 ~한 이래로
3 ~인지   4 ~한다면

Ready for Exams
p. 111

1 ②   2 ②
3 was so interesting that I couldn't stop reading it

해설

1 ・조건을 나타내는 접속사 if: '만약 ~한다면'
・명사절을 이끄는 접속사 if: '~인지 (아닌지)'
2 [보기]에 사용된 as는 '~하면서'의 뜻으로 while의 의미에
가깝다. (・나는 길을 걸으면서 콧노래를 불렀다. ・우리가 집
을 나설 때 전화가 울렸다.)
① 같은 정도나 양으로 (그 상황은 네가 보는 것만큼 나쁘지
않다.)
② 동시에; ~하는 동안에 (나는 집으로 달려오다가 얼음에
미끄러졌다.)
③ ~한 이유로; ~하기 때문에 (나는 지쳤기 때문에 일찍 잠
자리에 들었다.)
④ 같은 방식이나 방법으로 (로마에서는 로마인들이 하는 대
로 해라.)
⑤ 비록 ~일지라도 (그 작가가 위대했을지라도, 그는 나쁜 인
간임이 증명되었다.)
3 so ~ that+주어+cannot …(너무 ~해서 …할 수 없다) 구
문을 쓰되 과거 시제이므로 couldn't를 쓴다.

Review Test
p. 112

01 ③   02 ④
03 ⑤   04 ④
05 ④   06 ③
07 ②   08 ①
09 I don't know if[whether] she will like this
decision.
10 Neither you nor Chris seems to
11 (1) selfish as well as arrogant
(2) not only arrogant but also selfish
12 so
13 Although[Though, Even though]
14 Unless he listens to others

15 ⓑ Despite → Although[Though, Even though]
(또는 she had no experience → her lack of
experience)
16 She locked the door so that nobody could come
in.
17 will come → comes

해설

01 Neither A nor B: A와 B 둘 다 아닌 / either A or B: A
와 B 둘 중 하나 / as soon as: ~하자마자 / not only A
but also B: A뿐 아니라 B도
02 '그가 나를 떠난다 할지라도 나는 그를 사랑할 것이다.'라는
뜻이 되어야 자연스러우므로 even if가 알맞다.
03 ⑤의 if는 명사절을 이끄는 접속사로 '~인지 (아닌지)'의 뜻이
다. 나머지는 모두 조건을 나타내는 접속사로 쓰였다. (① 내
가 너의 자전거를 타도 되니? ② Bill은 그가 원한다면 모두
A를 받을 수 있다고 말한다. ③ 제가 지금 놀게 허락해주시면
밤새 공부할게요. ④ 내가 오늘 저녁에 영화 보러 가도 되니?
⑤ 네가 그것을 할 수 있는지 모르겠다.)
04 ⓒ if가 '만약 ~한다면'이라고 해석될 때 미래 대신 현재형을
쓴다. (will save → saves)
05 ①의 as, ②의 because, ③과 ⑤의 since는 '~하기 때문에'
로 쓰였지만 ④의 since는 '~한 이후로'의 의미이다.
06 빈칸에는 양보의 접속사가 들어가는 것이 적절하다. while은
'~하는 동안'이라는 뜻 외에도 '~한 반면[한편]'이라는 양보
를 나타내는 접속사로 사용되므로 가능하다.
07 ②는 명사절, ①, ③, ④, ⑤는 부사절로 쓰였다.
08 [보기]와 ①에서 As는 이유(~하기 때문에)를 나타내는 접속
사이다. ② ③ ④ '~하면서, ~함에 따라' ⑤ '~ 할 때'
09 명사절로 사용된 if[whether]절에서는 미래 시제를 써서 미
래를 표현한다.
10 neither A nor B(A와 B 둘 다 아닌)에서는 B에 동사를 일
치시키므로 seems가 알맞다.
11 B as well as A = not only A but also B: A뿐만 아니
라 B도
12 각각 결과와 목적을 나타내는 so가 알맞다. (・나는 너무 기진
맥진해서 일에 집중할 수 없었다. ・유나는 전 세계를 여행하
기 위해 저축을 하고 있다.)
13 '비록 ~이지만'의 뜻을 갖는 양보의 접속사가 내용상 알맞다.
(・가족 내 갈등이 일어나기는 하지만, 그것은 사소한 일에 관
한 것이다. ・그녀는 결승에서 졌지만, 스스로 자랑스러웠다.)
14 if ~ not은 unless(만약 ~하지 않는다면)로 바꾸어 쓸 수
있다. not을 사용하지 말라고 했으므로 unless를 써야 한다.
15 ⓐ 시간을 나타내는 부사절에서는 현재 시제가 미래를 대신
한다. ⓑ despite 뒤에는 명사(구)가 와야 한다.
16 so that+주어+can+동사원형: '~이 …할 수 있도록'
17 시간의 부사절에서는 현재 시제가 미래를 대신한다.

시험 직전에 챙겨 보는 비법노트
p. 114

한눈에 쏙!
1 as well as   4 1) so   2) such

헷갈리지 말자!
1 You → She / she were → you was

2 That
3 in order that 또는 so that
4 such

1 Not only A but also B = B as well as A (A뿐만 아니라 B도)
2 he will come이라는 문장을 이끌어주는 접속사 that이 필요하다.
3 문장을 이끌어주는 접속사가 포함된 in order that 또는 so that이 알맞다.
4 「a+형용사+명사」 앞에 such가 알맞다.

CHAPTER 11
가정법

22 가정법 과거, 가정법 과거완료

Let's Check It Out   p. 117

A   1 wore   2 will
    3 couldn't   4 have bought
    5 wouldn't have had   6 Had it not been for

B   1 doesn't know / is   2 broke / paid
    3 were[was] / could look
    4 had taken / would have saved
    5 But for   6 Without

Ready for Exams   p. 118

1 ③   2 ⑤
3 If it were not for bees / what would happen
4 wouldn't have hit

1 현재 사실의 반대를 가정하는 가정법 과거 문장으로, If she were[was] really angry, she would yell at me.로 영작할 수 있다.
2 과거 사실의 반대를 가정하는 가정법 과거완료이므로, If절에는 had+p.p.가, 주절에는 would have+p.p.가 와야 한다.
3 현재 사실에 반대되는 가정으로, 가정법 과거 형식으로 배열하면 된다. '~이 없다면'이라는 표현으로 if it were not for를 쓴다.
4 If절에서 가정법 과거완료임을 알 수 있으므로 주절에는 would have+p.p. 형태로 쓴다.

23 I wish 가정법, as if 가정법

Let's Check It Out   p. 120

A   1 were   2 had had
    3 had seen   4 understood
    5 hadn't played

B   1 am / don't have   2 wish / had joined
    3 was / wasn't   4 In fact / isn't
    5 as if[though] / had attended

C   1 could read   2 had been born
    3 어색한 곳 없음   4 had happened
    5 wasn't

Ready for Exams   p. 121

1 ③   2 ②
3 wish / could get up
4 as if[though] / were[was]

1 I am sorry 직실법 현재(부정)는 I wish 가정법 과거(긍정)로 바꿀 수 있다.
2 as if 가정법 과거완료는 과거 사실과 반대되는 상황을 가정할 때 사용하므로 진희는 과거에 입원하지 않았음을 알 수 있다.
3 현재의 일에 대한 유감을 표현하고 있으므로 I wish 가정법 과거로 써야 한다.
4 여자가 마네킹이 진짜 사람인 것처럼 악수하고 있으므로 as if 가정법 과거 형태로 쓴다.

Review Test   p. 122

01 ②④   02 ③
03 ④   04 ③
05 ②   06 ③④
07 If I had the courage / I would talk to him
08 didn't practice
09 didn't go → hadn't gone
10 had been / wouldn't have played
11 Were it not for water
12 (that) Mr. Jackson didn't have enough time then
13 I wish we[I] didn't have the same meal
14 ⓐ fought → had fought
15 as if he didn't see[hear]

01 가정법 과거 문장으로 「If+주어+과거 동사 ~, 주어+ 조동사의 과거형+동사원형 …」 순으로 쓴다. 주어가 I일 때 be동사는 were 또는 was를 쓸 수 있다.
02 과거 사실과 반대되는 가정으로, 가정법 과거완료가 와야 한다.
03 과거 사실에 대한 반대의 상황을 가정하는 as if 가정법 과거완료이므로, In fact, Nick didn't see a ghost then.의

의미이다.

04 가정법 과거완료에서 if절에는 had+p.p.가 오므로 haven't done을 hadn't done으로 써야 한다.

05 과거 사실에 대한 유감을 표현하므로 I'm sorry 직설법 과거(부정) 또는 I wish 가정법 과거완료(긍정)로 쓰면 된다.

06 ③ hasn't heard → hadn't heard ④ didn't arrive → hadn't arrived

07 현재 사실과 반대되는 가정으로 가정법 과거를 쓴다.

08 I wish 가정법 과거완료(긍정)는 I'm sorry 직설법 과거(부정)로 전환할 수 있다.

09 가정법 과거완료에서 if절에는 had+p.p.가 온다.

10 과거 사실과 반대되는 가정으로 가정법 과거완료 형태(If+주어+had+p.p. ~, 주어+wouldn't have+p.p. …)가 와야 한다.

11 If it were not for에서 if가 도치되어 생략된 구문이다.

12 I wish 가정법 과거완료(긍정)는 I'm sorry 직설법 과거(부정)로 전환할 수 있다.

13 현재 사실에 대한 소망의 표현으로 I wish 가정법 과거로 쓴다. (남편: 여보, 우리 매일 같은 음식 먹지 않았으면 좋겠어요. 부인: 그럼 당신이 직접 요리하지 그래요?)

14 just now가 과거이므로 as if절에서는 가정법 과거완료로 써야 한다.

15 as if절이 과거인 경우, 주절이 과거이면 같은 시제를 나타낸다.

시험 직전에 챙겨 보는 **비법노트**   p. 124

> **한눈에 쏙!**
> **1** 1) 현재   **2** 1) 과거
> **3** 1) ~라면 좋을 텐데   2) I am sorry (that)
>   3) ~였다면 좋을 텐데   4) I am sorry (that)
> **4** 1) 마치 ~인 것처럼   2) 마치 ~였던 것처럼
>
> **헷갈리지 말자!**
> **1** would
> **2** wouldn't have gotten
> **3** hadn't gone
>
> **해설**
> **1** 가정법 과거로 과거 동사(knew)일 때는 조동사 would가 알맞다.
> **2** 가정법 과거완료(had worn)이므로 「wouldn't have +과거분사형」이 알맞다.
> **3** as if 다음에 과거 사실과 반대인 상황을 나타내므로 과거완료형 hadn't gone이 알맞다.

CHAPTER 12 특수 구문

24 강조, 생략

Let's Check It Out   p. 127

A   **1** do   **2** very
    3 did send

B   **1** was Benny   **2** It was a new phone
    3 yesterday / happened to see Chris

C   **1** 강조 구문   **2** 가주어-진주어 구문
    3 가주어-진주어 구문   **4** 강조 구문

D   **1** B: I'd love to (go), but I can't.
    2 Though (I was) tired, I decided to do what I had to (do).
    3 You need to throw away all the things (that) you don't need.
    4 You should have called the police when I told you to (call the police).
    5 Line dancing was started by women (who were) waiting to use the bathroom.

Ready for Exams   p. 128

1 ②   **2** ④ ⑤
3 It was Judy that[who] was studying in the library. 또는 It was Judy that[who(m)] I saw in the library.

해설

1 ②의 that은 진주어로 쓰인 명사절을 이끄는 접속사이고, 나머지는 모두 It was ~ that… 강조 구문이다.

2 ⓐ는 틀린 부분이 없다. ⓑ 동사를 강조하는 문장이고 과거 시제이므로 'did+동사원형'을 써야 한다. ⓒ It ~ that… 강조 구문에서 강조하는 대상이 사람이면 that 대신 who를 쓸 수 있다.

3 누구인지 강조하는 대답이 대화상 자연스러우므로 It is ~ that 사이에 강조할 말 Judy를 쓰고 나머지는 that 뒤에 쓴다.

25 도치

Let's Check It Out   p.130

A   **1** were some coins   **2** have I seen
    3 could she control

B   **1** Were she in my shoes

        2 is the second bathroom
        3 was he that   4 is he an actor
        5 stands the fountain

C   1 So am I   2 Neither can I
    3 Neither do I

Ready for Exams
p. 131

1 ④   2 ③
3 (1) Near the river lies a small village.
   (2) A small village lies near the river.
4 Though she was invited to the event, she
   couldn't attend it.

해설

1 부정어 never를 강조하여 문장 첫머리로 보내면 「부정어
   (never)+조동사(should)+주어+동사원형」의 어순이 된
   다. (우리는 평화 통일의 가능성을 결코 배제해서는 안 된다.)
2 「so+조동사+주어」의 형태로, 긍정의 진술을 부각시켜 '~
   또한 그러하다'의 뜻으로 쓴다. (새들, 비 그리고 바람은 일종
   의 음악을 만들어낸다. 바다 또한 그렇다.)
3 (1) 장소 부사구가 문장 앞에 나가면 「부사구+동사+주어」
       의 순서로 써야 한다.
   (2) 원래 문장대로 부사구를 문장 뒤로 보내 「주어+동사+부
       사구」의 순서로 쓰면 된다.
4 양보의 부사절에서 '주어+be동사'가 생략된 문장이다. 뒤 문
   장의 주어가 she이고 invited와 수동의 관계이므로 과거 시
   제로 일치시켜 she was로 쓰는 것이 알맞다.

Review Test
p. 132

01 ①   02 ④
03 ③   04 ②
05 ⑤   06 ②
07 ① ④   08 ② ⑤
09 yesterday that   10 which is
11 very
12 If they are used properly, robots can be very
   useful.
13 So did I
14 (1) I haven't either.
   (2) Neither have I.
15 Were I given a chance to date a celebrity

해설

01 It is/was ~ that... 강조 구문은 '바로 ~이다'로 해석한다.
   (필요는 사람들이 물건을 발명하게 만든다. → 사람들이 물건
   을 발명하게 만드는 것은 바로 필요이다.)
02 ④의 do는 '하다'라는 의미의 본동사이고, [보기]와 나머지 문
   장의 do는 일반동사를 강조하는 조동사이다. (나는 저 시끄러
   운 음악 때문에 네 말을 듣는 데 정말 어려움을 겪고 있다.)
03 I found her ID card on the bus.의 강조 구문으로 ⓐ는
   목적어, ⓑ는 부사구 ⓒ는 주어를 강조하고 있다. ⓓ는 found
   를 find로, ⓔ는 which를 that으로 고쳐야 한다.
04 ②는 It이 가주어이고 that 이하가 진주어인 가주어-진주어
   구문이다. 나머지는 모두 강조 구문이다.

05 ① 대부정사 ② 부사절에 반복되는 '주어+be동사' 생략 ③
   재귀대명사의 강조 용법 ④ '주격 관계대명사+be동사' 생략
   ⑤ pain이 아니라 life is를 생략할 수 있다.
06 앞의 상황과 같음을 나타낼 때는 「so+조동사+주어」의 표현
   을 쓴다. 주어가 3인칭이고 일반동사 현재이므로 does가 알
   맞다.
07 ⓐ 「장소 부사+동사+주어」의 순으로 올바른 문장이다. ⓑ
   주어가 대명사일 때는 도치하지 않는다.
08 「부정어+조동사(do)+주어+일반동사」, 또는 「주어+빈도부
   사+일반동사」 어순으로 쓴다.
09 It is/was ~ that 사이에 강조하려는 말을 넣고, '바로 ~이
   다'로 해석한다.
10 콤마 뒤에 있는 which is를 없애면 두 개의 명사(구)가 나란
   히 연결되는 동격 구문이 된다. (파리는 흥미진진한 도시이다.
   파리는 프랑스에서 가장 큰 도시이다. → 프랑스에서 가장 큰
   도시인 파리는 흥미진진한 도시이다.)
11 명사를 강조할 때는 명사 앞에 very를 쓴다. (나는 그를 만날
   생각만 해도 긴장된다.)
12 If절에서 '주어+be동사'가 생략되었다.
13 「so+조동사+주어」(~도 또한 그렇다) 구문을 쓰면 된다.
   enjoyed가 일반동사의 과거형이므로 did를 사용한다.
14 (1) 부정문에서 '또한, 역시'는 either로 나타낸다.
   (2) 「neither+조동사+주어」(~도 또한 그렇지 않다) 구문
       을 사용한다. 동사가 현재완료이므로 조동사 have를 사
       용한다.
15 현재 사실의 반대를 가정하는 가정법 과거이므로 과거 동사
   를 써야 하고, If I were given a chance ~에서 If를 생략
   하면 주어와 동사가 도치되어 Were I given a chance ~
   가 된다.

시험 직전에 챙겨 보는 비법노트
p. 134

한눈에 쏙!

1 1) do   2) does   3) did   4) very   5) 주어
   6) 목적어   7) 부사(구)   8) 완전한   9) 불완전한
2 1) 목적격   2) 주격   3) be동사   4) 주어
   5) be동사   6) 부정사   7) 강조
3 1) 동사   2) 주어   3) 조동사   4) be동사   5) 주어
   6) Were   7) 주어

헷갈리지 말자!

1 written   2 walking
3 has he trusted

해설

1 수식을 받는 menu가 쓰는 것이 아니라 쓰여지는 것이
   므로 written으로 고쳐야 한다. written 앞에는
   which[what] was가 생략된 것으로 볼 수 있다.
2 While we were walking에서 we were를 생략한
   것으로 walking으로 고쳐야 한다.
3 부정어구(Never)가 문장 앞으로 이동한 것으로 도치구
   문이다. 따라서 has he trusted로 고쳐야 한다.

MEMO

내신략공

중학영문법 3 개념이해책